The
Bridge
World
Magazine

SWISS MATCH CHALLENGE

By Jeff Rubens

LAWRENCE & LEONG PUBLISHING

Printed in the United States of America

Lawrence & Leong Publishing
10430 Greenview Drive
Oakland, California 94605

Library of Congress Catalog Card Number: 92-074745

ISBN 1-877908-05-3

Contents

Introduction

THE BEST WAY TO LEARN TO BID AND PLAY like a winner
is to have a successful player sit down beside you and
analyze your play of challenging deals. The next best way
is to practice on a book of this kind.

As you attack a problem you will be asked a question
at each key decision point. Decide your answer. Then
study the analysis that immediately follows and move
on. Whether you do well on any particular hand or
question is not the point. How you improve is what
counts. Improvement is virtually guaranteed to come
about through answering the questions with your own
reasons and understanding the solutions.

You will be given the opportunity to play several Swiss
matches as a member of a team of four players. While
you and your partner sit in one direction, your teammates will play sit in the opposite direction at the other
table. In each match the same set of seven boards will be
played at both tables. To find out how well you did, look
in the Post-Mortem that follows each match. For each
board you will add your score with your teammates' and
convert using the IMP table that follows on page two.

For example, if you, sitting North–South, bid and make
a vulnerable four–spade game for a score of plus 620 while
your teammates sitting East–West score minus 170
because their opponents bid only three spades making
four, your team wins a net total of 450 points, which
converts to 10 IMPs. The team with the most IMPs wins.

International Match Point Scale

Diff. in Pts.	IMPs	Diff. in Pts.	IMPs
20–40	1	750–890	13
50–80	2	900–1090	14
90–120	3	1100–1290	15
130–160	4	1300–1490	16
170–210	5	1500–1740	17
220–260	6	1750–1990	18
270–310	7	2000–2240	19
320–360	8	2250–2490	20
370–420	9	2500–2990	21
430–490	10	3000–3490	22
500–590	11	3500–3990	23
600–740	12	4000 and up	24

The bidding system you will be using is Bridge World Standard, a consensus system of leading American experts and thousands of Bridge World magazine readers. You need not know all the ins and outs of the system, only the basics: five–card majors with a forcing one–notrump response, negative doubles, strong one–notrump opening, Stayman, Jacoby transfers, limit raises, weak–two bids, weak jump overcalls; for slam bidding: Gerber, Roman Key–Card Blackwood, and splinters. Opening leads against suit contracts are third best from even, low from odd. All other leads are old fashioned. If any other conventions are involved they will be mentioned during the description of the deal.

On most deals the correct action will be the same regardless of the form of scoring. At times, your final action may be influenced by IMP scoring. As in rubber bridge, the emphasis at IMP scoring is on making and breaking the contract and on insuring against large adverse swings. Since the most you can lose on any one board is 24 IMPs, your team can still be in contention after a large adverse swing. For this reason, IMP scoring is popular among experts.

Ignore the tiny swings. Concentrate on making your contract instead of on overtricks. Play in your safest contract and not necessarily the highest ranking. If you bid six clubs when six spades also makes you will lose a very small swing. But if your opponents go down in six spades while you make six clubs the swing will be very large.

When competing for the part score be reluctant to be pushed higher when you already have a good chance of going plus. Be more conservative in bidding non-vulnerable games than vulnerable ones. Small slams need a fifty percent chance or better. It is better to avoid bidding a doubtful grand slam as a small slam may be already a good score.

The deals were created to mimic real life situations. Sometimes, one small slip up anywhere will cost the match; other times, there will be so many points flying about that all you need do is avoid too many gross blunders. Mostly, it will be somewhere in between.

As in real life, you can be unlucky. You may get to a great contract but the cards may not break normally. You may have taken the best percentage line to make your contract but the inferior line would have worked. Worse yet, your opponents may make a truly silly decision that gets richly rewarded. Bridge can be a frustrating game at times. However, plug away and do your best. In the long run good judgment should win out.

Good luck!

Match One

Sleepwalk

YOU'VE INVESTED A LOT OF TIME in an extended–weekend Regional, and it has paid off; things are going nicely. First, and foremost, you are playing well and know it. Second, this has shown up decently in the results: a section top in the Mixed (and you'd have placed well overall but for two slams on finesses— yours down, theirs made—in the second session): fifth overall in the Masters' Pairs: third overall in the Open Pairs.

You've got a decent team of straightforward Bridge World Standard types for the Swiss, but there is some question as to whether you will be at your best. Along with the good results, you've been staying up late post–morteming. When you get to your table for the first match, you are yawning. Will you be slumbering through this event?

The first match looks easy enough. Your youthful opponents, who seem not to have been staying up late, are bright, cheerful and friendly as they introduce themselves. And they play no fancy conventions. How good can they be? Of course, one must always remember the important advice, "Never trust anybody under thirty."

You think you heard your partner tell you that three imps is needed for a full win; if so, a win by one or two imps will give your team three–quarters of a point. However, you aren't sure what he said and are not about to ask—you don't want to reveal that you haven't fully woken up yet. (Yawn!)

Board 1

Partner is the dealer
None vulnerable

DUMMY (RHO)
♠ 10983
♡ 54
◇ KJ7
♣ AQ62

YOU
♠ AQJ764
♡ AK6
◇ 5
♣ 1087

PARTNER	RHO	YOU	LHO
Pass	Pass	1♠	3◇ [1]
3♠	5◇	Double	Pass
Pass	Pass		

[1] Preemptive

Partner leads the heart queen.

Plan your defense.

```
                    NORTH
                    ♠ K52
                    ♡ QJ109
                    ◊ 83
                    ♣ KJ53
    WEST                          EAST
    ♠ —                           ♠ 10983
    ♡ 8732                        ♡ 54
    ◊ AQ109642                    ◊ KJ7
    ♣ 94                          ♣ AQ62
                    SOUTH
                    ♠ AQJ764
                    ♡ AK6
                    ◊ 5
                    ♣ 1087
```

There are no tricks for the defense in spades. And there is nothing to be done about clubs—what's there is there. So, the only situation that is in doubt is in hearts. If declarer started with four cards in hearts, the defense must play two rounds of trumps in order to stop the second ruff. Since you cannot lead the second round of trumps yourself, you must overtake the queen of hearts at trick one, shift to a trump, and stand ready to play low on the second round of hearts so that partner can lead a second trump. You're not quite done even then— when declarer takes one heart ruff, ruffs a spade, and runs diamonds, you must cling to your three clubs as long as dummy holds that many (else partner will be squeezed between hearts and clubs).

Results

If you defended correctly, plus 100; otherwise, minus 550.

Board 2

East dealer
North–South vulnerable

You, South, hold:

♠AJ1054 ♡KQJ4 ◇A8 ♣KQ

SOUTH	WEST	NORTH	EAST
—	—	—	Pass
1♠	Pass	4◇ [1]	Double
4NT	Pass	5♣ [2]	Pass
5◇	Pass	5♡ [3]	Pass
6♠	7◇	Double	Pass
?			

[1] Splinter
[2] Zero or three key cards
[3] Denies spade queen

What call do you make?

```
                    NORTH
                    ♠ K982
                    ♡ A875
                    ♢ 4
                    ♣ A943
    WEST                            EAST
    ♠ 3                             ♠ Q76
    ♡ 9632                          ♡ 10
    ♢ J7632                         ♢ KQ1095
    ♣ J52                           ♣ 10876
                    SOUTH
                    ♠ AJ1054
                    ♡ KQJ4
                    ♢ A8
                    ♣ KQ
```

When staying out of seven was going to be worth 1430, it made sense. However, once East–West have sacrificed, staying out of seven may be worth significantly less. You know East–West have ten diamonds, so the penalty may be only 1400 or 1100. In the latter case, you will lose 8 imps, a healthy chunk, if your teammates don't find the sacrifice.

Under these circumstances, it is better to bid seven and try to find the spade queen. If you do go on to seven, you should bid it in notrump; then, you can run side winners before committing yourself in spades. With any luck, the fall of cards in the round suits will give you a clue to the location of the spade queen.

Results

If you passed the double, plus 1400; if you bid seven spades, minus 100, if you bid seven notrump, plus 2220.

Are you awake yet? If not, you should be in just a moment . . .

Board 3

South dealer
East–West vulnerable

As South, you hold:

♠ 43　♡ AK　◇ AK94　♣ AKJ108

The bidding proceeds:

SOUTH	NORTH
1♣	1♠
2◇	2♠
3NT	4♣
4♡	4♠
6♣	7♣
Pass	

Do you agree with one club?

We like one club. We are not deterred by the stopperless spade suit from opening two notrump, or even two clubs (then two notrump). But if we choose that route, how are we ever going to show those powerful clubs and diamonds, to investigate possible contracts in those suits? By opening one club, we may be able to reveal both suits, then the power (see actual sequence), leaving partner options.

One club has risks, of course. It might pass out there when we can make game. But how likely is that? Partner will rarely pass. If he passes and is short in clubs, we may well belong out of game. If he passes and is not short in clubs, there is little chance that East will pass it out. All things considered, our chance of passing out a game is slight.

11

DUMMY
♠ AK8762
♡ 954
◇ J10
♣ Q3

YOU
♠ 43
♡ AK
◇ AK94
♣ AKJ108

West leads the club four (drat him!).

Plan the play.

```
                    NORTH
                    ♠ AK8762
                    ♡ 954
                    ◊ J10
                    ♣ Q3
WEST                                    EAST
♠ J5                                    ♠ Q109
♡ Q10863                                ♡ J72
◊ Q73                                   ◊ 8652
♣ 642                                   ♣ 975
                    SOUTH
                    ♠ 43
                    ♡ AK
                    ◊ AK94
                    ♣ AKJ108
```

The diamond finesse is roughly a 50–50 proposition. Is it better than even–money to ruff a diamond in dummy, and then, if the queen of diamonds is still at large, to hope for a squeeze?

Only a rough calculation is necessary. (We'll use numbers fairly close to the real ones and avoid repeating "approximately" in all the places it is needed.) Diamonds will break four–three some 62% of the time. Three–sevenths of that time (27%), the queen will drop. Of the remainder (35%), the squeeze will work less than half the time—let's guess 15% of that 35% , bringing the total to 42%. When diamonds are five–two (31%), the queen drops two–sevenths of the time (8%), which already gets us up to about 50%, plus the squeeze chances here, plus singleton queen of diamonds, plus some little dribbles . . . The squeeze just has to be superior.

Results

Finesse, minus 50; squeeze plus 1440. Little things sometimes mean a lot. (Are you still drowsy? Don't slump in your chair—there's more action on the way!)

Board 4

West dealer
Both vulnerable

You, South, hold:

♠ KJ6   ♡ A2   ◇ AKQJ83   ♣ J6

SOUTH	NORTH
—	1♣
2◇	2♠
3◇	4◇
4♡	4♠
5♠	6♣
?	

What call do you make?

```
                    NORTH
                    ♠ A832
                    ♡ J8
                    ◇ 62
                    ♣ AK843
WEST                                    EAST
♠ Q107                                  ♠ 954
♡ 10973                                 ♡ KQ542
◇ 107                                   ◇ 954
♣ 10762                                 ♣ Q9
                    SOUTH
                    ♠ KJ6
                    ♡ A6
                    ◇ AKQJ83
                    ♣ J5
```

Considering all the evidence—partner never made a
discouraging noise; he was willing to cooperate in bidding to higher and higher levels—there must be some
play for seven diamonds. Probably, at worst it could be
on a three–three club break. And any significant extra
value in partner's hand will make seven excellent—
even imponderable extras, such as the tens of spades or
diamonds. Furthermore, if seven does not make maybe
six will not make either (since, presumably, a heart lead
against six will bare a loser). Under these circumstances, you don't need to wait for the usual chance
before bidding seven profitably.

Based on previous results, you might welcome a tie
result on this potentially swingy board. Unfortunately,
you can't tell whether the opponents are more likely to
reach six or seven.

Results

If you bid six diamonds, minus 100 (if you made it go
back to sleep): if you bid six notrump, minus 200 (if you

bid or made it, go back to sleep); if you bid seven diamonds, minus 200; if you bid seven notrump, why?

Enough excitement to wake you up? Not yet? Well then . . .

Board 5

Partner is the dealer
Your side vulnerable

```
                    DUMMY (LHO)
                    ♠ A3
                    ♡ 82
                    ◇ K87
                    ♣ AJ9642
        YOU
        ♠ 10987
        ♡ Q953
        ◇ 62
        ♣ 1073
```

YOU	LHO	PARTNER	RHO
—	—	Pass	2NT
Pass	6NT	Pass	Pass
Pass			

You lead the spade ten. Here is fair warning—you are going to be embarrassed if you are sleepy on this deal, so right now while declarer looks things over it would be wise for you to . . .

Plan your defense.

```
                    NORTH
                    ♠ 6542
                    ♡ J76
                    ◇ 9543
                    ♣ KQ
WEST                                        EAST
♠ A3                                        ♠ KQJ
♡ 82                                        ♡ AK104
◇ K87                                       ◇ AQJ10
♣ AJ9642                                    ♣ 85
                    SOUTH
                    ♠ 10987
                    ♡ Q953
                    ◇ 62
                    ♣ 1073
```

The club suit looks to be critical. An "interesting" situation can arise only if declarer is missing the queen or the king–queen. If he plays king and another, you should sometimes play the ten and sometimes not. You need not worry about how you handle it any one particular time (and your choice is not likely to have any effect on a competent declarer anyway).

However, if declarer starts with a finesse of the nine, or the equivalent, so that he may be missing king–queen, you must be on your toes. By the second round of clubs you must get that ten of clubs out of your hand. If you don't, you won't like the result. Suppose the play goes, first, a club to the nine and queen (or king). On the second club, if you play low declarer will realize that he cannot pick up the suit when you started with honor ten–fourth; he will go up with the ace on the second round, his only chance.

Even if declarer might find value in making only two club tricks (e.g., switch the heart ten and heart jack in the diagram—declarer can use two fast club tricks since he then has a heart finesse for twelve tricks), you should still play the club ten on the second round. That will ensure a second finesse, and the defeat of the contract.

Results

If you were ready with the club ten, plus 50; otherwise minus 990.

Board 6

East dealer
East–West vulnerable

NORTH(DUMMY)
♠ J543
♡ KQJ
♢ AKQ
♣ KJ9

SOUTH
♠ AQ10
♡ 9865
♢ 108
♣ A1064

SOUTH	WEST	NORTH	EAST
—	—	—	Pass
Pass	1♠[1]	Double	2♠
2NT	Pass	6NT	Pass
Pass	Pass		

[1] Never trust anybody under thirty.

Do you agree with two notrump?

Nobody has any idea what to do in this sort of position—
it's not worth worrying about. On the technical side, the
spade ten is an indicator in favor of two notrump over,
say, three hearts or three clubs.

The play proceeds:

> Diamond seven, **queen**, five, eight.
> Spade three, six, **queen**, two.
> Heart five, seven, **jack**, two.
> Heart **king**, three, six, diamond two.
> Diamond **ace**, jack, ten, three.
> Diamond **king**, heart four, heart eight, four.
> Spade four, seven, **ten**, eight.

So far, so good. Now what?

NORTH
♠ J543
♡ KQJ
◇ AKQ
♣ KJ9

WEST
♠ 82
♡ 7
◇ 976432
♣ Q832

EAST
♠ K976
♡ A10432
◇ J5
♣ 75

SOUTH
♠ AQ10
♡ 9865
◇ 108
♣ A1064

You should play West for the queen of clubs. If spades are three–three, then so are the clubs—either opponent might have the queen. But that card would give East 10 HCP plus a fit; would he have made his single raise? Surely he would instead have redoubled, planning to follow with two spades. And if spades are four–two, West has four clubs to East's two; moreover, East would certainly not have contented himself with two spades holding,

♠ Kxxx ♡ A10xx ◊ Jx ♣ Qx

Since you are going to play West for the club queen regardless, make sure you pick up the clubs. Lead the club ten (if it is covered, win three clubs in dummy, spade ace, club ace), play a club to the jack, club king, spade ace, club ace.

Results

If you played it that way, plus 1440, or plus 660 if you wouldn't have bid two notrump; if you guessed clubs but blocked them, minus 100; otherwise, minus 200.

Board 7

South dealer
Both vulnerable

You, South, hold:

♠ Q86 ♡ AJ7 ◊ AJ9765 ♣ 2

SOUTH	WEST	NORTH	EAST
1◊	3♠	Pass	3NT
Pass	Pass	Pass	

What is your opening lead?

```
              NORTH
              ♠ 1075
              ♡ Q9532
              ◊ 4
              ♣ 9654
WEST                              EAST
♠ AKJ9432                         ♠ —
♡ 1086                            ♡ K4
◊ 32                              ◊ KQ108
♣ 3                               ♣ AKQJ1087
              SOUTH
              ♠ Q86
              ♡ AJ7
              ◊ AJ9765
              ♣ 2
```

You face a tough guess and any particular layout proves nothing. You shold do what analysis you can, and hope for the best. Your spade holding suggests that East is not bidding on a fit. Probably he has clubs, with high cards in the reds. Does your partner have the diamond king, in which case your side might be able to run diamonds, or do your best chances lie in hearts? It's a guess. We'd go for hearts, on this theory: if East has a borderline hand, the heart suit may be wide open (with East able to take a lot of clubs plus West's spade ace–king). We'd lead the ace of hearts (intending to try diamonds if partner discourages), in the hope of being able to run the entire suit. With the cards shown in the diagram, we'd be wrong, but we'd wind up right. Some people have all the luck! And the result of this lead is just luck, whichever way it turns out. You must accept the fact that not every bridge situation can be calculated down to the last iota.

Results

If you led a high heart, plus 100; if you led spade or a club minus 600; if you led a diamond, minus 630.

Post–Mortem

Board 1

Where careful defense was required to defeat five diamonds doubled, the line of defense was unimportant in the other room.

NORTH
♠ K52
♡ QJ109
◇ 83
♣ KJ53

WEST
♠ —
♡ 8732
◇ AQ109642
♣ 94

EAST
♠ 10983
♡ 54
◇ KJ7
♣ AQ62

SOUTH
♠ AQJ764
♡ AK6
◇ 5
♣ 1087

SOUTH	WEST	NORTH	EAST
—	—	Pass	Pass
1♠	3◇	3♠	4◇
4♠	5◇	5♠	Pass
Pass	Pass		

West led the ace of diamonds (three, seven, five), studied, and found the club shift. North–South minus 50.

Board 2

Where you had to decide whether to bid seven, and which seven, over an opposing sacrifice, the players with your cards (unlike their teammates) were using a few fancy conventions. Where you started one spade—four diamonds as a splinter raise, they started one spade—four clubs to show a spade raise with short diamonds. (Perhaps they read Verne Smith's article on "Switched Splinters" in The Bridge World.) Your teammates did not enter the auction, and South, finding he was missing four spades to the queen, settled for six spades.

North–South plus 1430.

Board 3

Where you had to decide between a simple diamond finesse and a ruffout–plus–squeeze–chance at seven clubs, the player with your cards reached six notrump (after a two–notrump opening). Declarer lost a diamond finesse and took 12 tricks.

North–South plus 990.

Board 4

Where you had to decide whether to bid six diamonds or seven diamonds, the player in your seat played it fancy.

NORTH
♠ A832
♡ J8
◇ 62
♣ AK843

WEST
♠ Q107
♡ 10973
◇ 107
♣ 10762

EAST
♠ 954
♡ KQ542
◇ 954
♣ Q9

SOUTH
♠ KJ6
♡ A6
◇ AKQJ83
♣ J5

West led the ten of hearts against South's contract of six diamonds. Declarer ducked in dummy, won the heart ace, drew trumps pitching a spade from dummy, played ace–king and another club, ruffing, and then exited with a heart. East won and played another heart—ruffed, dummy discarding a club. Finally, declarer played his last trump, throwing a spade from dummy, then a spade to the ace and a spade finesse. North South minus 200.

How do you evaluate South's play?

A mild insult to the opponents. He assumed they might help him decide between the finesse and the squeeze. But the result was that he finessed in a position where being wrong cost him an extra 100 points.

Board 5

Where the play of the club suit was critical in a slam,

DUMMY
♣ AJ9642

DEFENDER
♣ 1073

DEFENDER
♣ KQ

DECLARER
♣ 85

the defender with your ten–seven–three was careful to play his ten on the second round, so declarer duly went down. (And they say young people aren't getting a good education nowadays! You can't believe everything you read in the papers.)

North–South plus 50.

Board 6

Where you had to guess the queen of clubs to make six notrump, your opposite numbers bid two notrump—three notrump without interference, and took eleven tricks after a heart lead.

North–South plus 660.

Board 7

Where you had to guess the lead against three notrump, your teammate overpreempted four spades with the West cards . . .

```
                    NORTH
                    ♠ 1075
                    ♡ Q9532
                    ◊ 4
                    ♣ 9654
WEST                                    EAST
♠ AKJ9432                               ♠ —
♡ 1086                                  ♡ K4
◊ 32                                    ◊ KQ108
♣ 3                                     ♣ AKQJ1087
                    SOUTH
                    ♠ Q86
                    ♡ AJ7
                    ◊ AJ9765
                    ♣ 2
```

SOUTH	WEST	NORTH	EAST
1◊	4♠	Pass	Pass
Pass			

Against four spades, the defense started with a
diamond and a diamond ruff. North shifted to a small
heart and declarer put up dummy's king (which was not
smart). The defense took heart ace, heart queen–jack;
then a diamond. West ruffed with the spade nine (which
was not smart), so the defense took two spade tricks to
go with three hearts and two diamonds.

North–South plus 400.

□   □   □

Should you tell your Westmate to get more sleep? How
did you do in your sleepy condition? Whether you won
or lost, certainly these deals should have helped you
wake up!

27

Match Two

Experts Lose Also

YOU HAD AN UNLUCKY FIRST ROUND. It was unlucky that the opponents bid and made a game that needed a finesse and a three–two break: it was unlucky that your teammate went down in a part–score he should have made; it was unlucky that you and partner misdefended a game that wasn't reached in the other room. You need a margin of 3 imps for a full win in the seven–board matches in this Regional Swiss (you get three–quarters for winning by 1 or 2 imps), and you lost by more than three times that much.

Unluckier yet, your second–round opponent is a group of experts who also managed to lose their first match. If your team starts off with two losses, it is likely to enter a state of depression that will make you wish you had stayed home to watch football. However, the unfavorable draw also provides an opportunity—if your group can rise up and smite the favorites. The morale boost should carry you through the day. And that will be an achievement independent or your standing in the tournament.

The opponents arrive, and methods are announced. You and your partner are pretty much "book" players. The experts have a great number of special exceptions and footnotes listed on their convention card, but on analysis their methods look like Bridge World Standard to you.

Board 8

LHO is the dealer
None vulnerable

                        DUMMY(RHO)
                        ♠ 53
                        ♡ QJ9
                        ◇ K10863
                        ♣ J65

                                        YOU
                                        ♠ AQ76
                                        ♡ AK65
                                        ◇ Q9754
                                        ♣ —

LHO	PARTNER	RHO	YOU
5♣	Pass	Pass	Double
Pass	Pass	Pass	

The play proceeds:

> *Diamond two, three, four,* ***jack***
> *Club two,* ***ace****, five, ?*

What do you discard?

NORTH
♠ 9842
♡ 1087432
◇ 2
♣ A3

WEST
♠ KJ10
♡ —
◇ AJ
♣ KQ1098742

EAST
♠ 53
♡ QJ9
◇ K10863
♣ J65

SOUTH
♠ AQ76
♡ AK65
◇ Q9754
♣ —

Should the card South played on the first trick; be a suit–preference signal? This is the normal interpretation when partner is trying for a ruff, but this situation is tricky. It cannot be clear to North, from the appearance of dummy, that South knows that the lead was a singleton. South does know, but only because of the cards he holds.

Be that as it may, you should now give as unmistakable a signal as possible for spades. North might have left in five clubs doubled with six hearts to the ten, but he would surely have taken out holding the club ace plus either 11 major–suit cards, or seven spades to the king jack–ten. Therefore, you know absolutely that a spade lead from partner followed by a diamond ruff will sink the contract— cashing out correctly for extra undertricks is secondary.

Therefore, you should discard something at trick two that shrieks for spades. The queen of spades and the queen of diamonds are the leading candidates.

Results

If you got partner to lead a spade, plus 100; otherwise minus 550.

Board 9

North dealer
East–West vulnerable

You, South, hold:

♠ 87   ♡ AKQJ104   ◇ 965   ♣ 32

SOUTH	WEST	NORTH	EAST
—	—	1♣	Pass
1♡	Pass	1♠	Pass
3♡	Pass	3NT	Pass
?			

What call do you make?

```
                    NORTH
                  ♠ AQ64
                  ♡ 3
                  ◊ K87
                  ♣ KQ874
    WEST                          EAST
  ♠ J1092                       ♠ K53
  ♡ 9652                        ♡ 87
  ◊ AJ3                         ◊ Q1042
  ♣ 105                         ♣ AJ96
                    SOUTH
                  ♠ 87
                  ♡ AKQJ104
                  ◊ 965
                  ♣ 32
```

Three notrump could be a horrible contract. If partner has a good hand with a heart void, he can hardly bid otherwise; yet three notrump will be a candidate for hideous contract of the year.

Nonetheless, we believe that passing three notrump is best. With those solid hearts, you can make it opposite bare minimum hands. And your third diamond is good for notrump also, a diamond the opponents don't have.

Results

If you passed, plus 400. (Partner is good enough to make three notrump even against tough defense.) If you took out to four hearts, minus 50 (they are good enough to beat four hearts even though you will play it well).

Board 10

RHO is the dealer
Both vulnerable

DUMMY (LHO)
♠ —
♡ A973
♢ 54
♣ KQJ10862

YOU
♠ AKJ
♡ 10642
♢ Q987
♣ 53

RHO	YOU	LHO	PARTNER
1♡	Pass	3♠[1]	Pass
3NT[2]	Pass	4♡[3]	Pass
6♡	Pass	Pass	Pass

[1] Heart raise: unspecified void
[2] Which void?
[3] Spades

The play proceeds:

> *Spade king, **heart three**, two, nine.*
> *Club king, ace, **heart five**, ?*

Plan your defense.

```
                    NORTH
                    ♠ 8765432
                    ♡ —
                    ◇ 106
                    ♣ A974
        WEST                        EAST
        ♠ —                         ♠ Q109
        ♡ A973                      ♡ KQJ85
        ◇ 54                        ◇ AKJ32
        ♣ KQJ10862                  ♣ —
                    SOUTH
                    ♠ AKJ
                    ♡ 10642
                    ◇ Q987
                    ♣ 53
```

Very fancy bidding! But don't be distracted—it seems declarer has made a mistake. Maybe those experts aren't quite as good as they are supposed to be. They blunder sometimes, just like the rest of us. The only real difference is that they do it less often. If you want to have a chance to beat them, you must realize that they will make mistakes—be prepared to take advantage.

What has happened on this deal? Declarer, whose hand undoubtedly resembles the one shown in the diagram. will play a high trump expecting to draw trumps and take the rest. The four–zero trump break will put a crimp in those plans. However, you must be ready to play the ten of hearts if declarer next leads his last remaining "low" trump. (If you don't, declarer can finesse dummy's heart nine, throw a spade on a high club and pitch his last spade on another high club while you ruff—he can then draw trumps from dummy, and take the rest.)

Declarer has lots of options after he sees the four–zero trump break. One possibility is that he will put you to the test by playing the eight of hearts; if you play your ten, he will win in dummy and go for diamonds, hoping for a three–three break or doubleton queen (or, he may try the diamond finesse). When that fails to materialize he will be down two.

Results

If you were ready, plus 200; if not, minus 1430.

Board 11

South dealer
None vulnerable

NORTH
♠ QJ85
♡ A32
♦ 106
♣ K974

SOUTH
♠ A
♡ QJ9
♦ K7543
♣ QJ108

SOUTH	WEST	NORTH	EAST
1♦	Pass	1♠	Pass
2♣	Pass	3♣	Pass
Pass	Pass		

West leads the heart ten.

Plan the play.

NORTH
♠ QJ85
♡ A32
♢ 106
♣ K974

WEST
♠ K9764
♡ 10
♢ QJ82
♣ A53

EAST
♠ 1032
♡ K87654
♢ A9
♣ 62

SOUTH
♠ A
♡ QJ9
♢ K7543
♣ QJ108

Even if you could afford to draw trumps, which you can't, it is wildly improbable that you can stop the opponents from getting a heart ruff. So concede that (mentally), and budget for the opponents to win one heart, one heart ruff and the ace of trumps. If they get two diamonds you are down, so you need to find the diamond ace onside: you don't want to draw trumps too early—the opponents' heart ruff will probably take care of any trump–handling problems that were scheduled to develop.

It is often good technique to break the opponents transportation to make it hard for them to get a ruff, or do other nastiness. Here, however, there is no special advantage to destroying the East–West entry in hearts (they have others anyway), and ducking the first trick exposes you to the risk, admittedly small but nonetheless present, of two heart ruffs. So, you should grab dummy's ace of hearts, lead a diamond to the king, and let nature take its course. (You will not, of course, ruff any diamond with dummy's four of clubs.)

Results

If you ducked the first trick, or if you did not lead diamonds early from dummy, minus 50: otherwise, plus 110.

Board 12

West dealer
North–South vulnerable

You, South, hold:

♠ 643　♡ AKQ109　◇ KJ　♣ 984

SOUTH	WEST	NORTH	EAST
—	Pass	Pass	Pass
1♡	1♠	2♠[1]	Pass
?			

[1] Too strong to raise to two hearts

What call do you make?

This is a borderline decision. The total value of your hand is mediocre, and there are a lot of possible losers, but the trumps are strong. Since partner doesn't have good trumps, he must have sound high–card values or spade shortness. You can hope for a decent mesh.

Another factor influencing this decision is the scoring and the vulnerability. Aggressive game bidding is rewarded when you are vulnerable at IMPs—unless you occasionally get doubled and go for a bundle. Considering your trumps, you aren't going to get doubled, so all the indications are to be aggressive.

We'll assume you bid four hearts, and all pass.

DUMMY
♠ J7
♡ 875
◇ Q1085
♣ AKQ10

YOU
♠ 643
♡ AKQ109
◇ KJ
♣ 984

The play proceeds:

> *Spade **king**, seven, ten, three.*
> *Spade **ace**, jack, eight, four.*
> *Spade queen, **heart eight**, five, nine.*

Plan the play.

                    NORTH
                    ♠ J7
                    ♡ 875
                    ◇ Q1085
                    ♣ AKQ10
WEST   EAST
♠ AKQ92   ♠ 1085
♡ 4   ♡ J632
◇ 74   ◇ A9632
♣ 76532   ♣ J
                    SOUTH
                    ♠ 643
                    ♡ AKQ109
                    ◇ KJ
                    ♣ 984

East has gone out of his way to get the third spade played; he didn't even know his partner held the queen. It couldn't have been because he was afraid partner would blow a trick by shifting to diamonds—you know East has that ace. Either East has four or five hearts to the jack and is trying to arrange a trump trick for himself, or he is engaged in a sneaky doublecross.

We bet against the doublecross. Why should East risk discouraging partner from playing diamonds? Why should East's extravagant spade play (probably a mistake anyway, compared to getting the diamond shift and leading a third spade himself) even occur to him unless he has a possible trump trick?

Once you have decided to finesse in hearts, you might as well finesse on the first round. This gains some of the time when East has five trumps, and loses when West has singleton jack—but the latter combination is excluded by your assumption regarding East's tactics.

Results

If you finessed against the jack of hearts on the first or second rounds of hearts, plus 620 (or plus 170 if you bid no higher than three hearts—partner, with very weak trumps, will probably decline any invitation, even three clubs); otherwise, minus 100 (or plus 140)

Board 13

North dealer
Both vulnerable

You, South, hold:

♠ KJ865   ♡ A7   ◇ 1043   ♣ 542

SOUTH	WEST	NORTH	EAST
—	—	1NT	2♡
2♠	3♡	Pass	Pass
?			

What call do you make?

```
                    NORTH
                    ♠ Q3
                    ♥ 1042
                    ◊ AQJ9
                    ♣ AK86
    WEST                            EAST
    ♠ A10972                        ♠ 4
    ♥ Q5                            ♥ KJ9863
    ◊ 8652                          ◊ K7
    ♣ 107                           ♣ QJ93
                    SOUTH
                    ♠ KJ865
                    ♥ A7
                    ◊ 1043
                    ♣ 542
```

There is no reason for you to do anything dramatic. In the long run, pass will be best. Partner won't have three spades unless he has weak offense and good defense, in which case passing three hearts should be right; probably, he has three hearts. You should have at least as good a chance to set three hearts as to make three spades (or anything else).

Three hearts is unlikely to be hurt badly, so there is no cause to double (since if the lie is lucky for East–West they may make it, and you lose a lot, whereas you gain little by doubling unless you beat them two tricks). Similarly, no great harm is likely to come to three spades, but it might get doubled on an unlucky day. In any event that does not represent your best chance for a plus.

Results

If you passed, minus 140: if you doubled, minus 730; if you bid three spades, minus 200; if you bid three notrump (surely you didn't!), minus 800.

Board 14

East dealer
None vulnerable

You, South, hold:

♠ KQ9862   ♡ 5   ◇ AQJ   ♣ 1098

SOUTH	WEST	NORTH	EAST
—	—	—	Pass
1♠	1NT[1]	2♠	4♡
4♠	5♡	Pass	Pass
Pass			

[1] 17–20

What is your opening lead?

```
              NORTH
              ♠ J743
              ♡ A632
              ◇ 753
              ♣ 42
WEST                          EAST
♠ A10                         ♠ 5
♡ K8                          ♡ QJ10974
◇ K642                        ◇ 1098
♣ AKJ73                       ♣ Q65
              SOUTH
              ♠ KQ9862
              ♡ 5
              ◇ AQJ
              ♣ 1098
```

North and East must be bidding on distributional strength, so a spade lead is unlikely to set up a trick for the defense. Furthermore, East must have some heart honors in his long suit, so he is unlikely to hold the king of diamonds. If West or North holds the king of diamonds, it must be best to lead that suit: even in the unlikely event that East holds the diamond king, you may break even by leading diamonds. All things considered, the diamond lead stands out.

Which diamond to lead? That is less clear. There is probably little danger of cutting the link with partner should he hold a doubleton (it is almost certain you'll have to be given your diamond tricks anyway). However, an advantage to leading the queen is that partner may hold the ten and declarer may duck twice in dummy.

Results

If you led diamonds, plus 50; if not, minus 450.

Post–Mortem

Board 8

Where you had to maneuver a diamond ruff for partner to defeat five clubs doubled, the bidding started lower at the other table.

NORTH
♠ 9842
♡ 1087432
◇ 2
♣ A3

WEST
♠ KJ10
♡ —
◇ AJ
♣ KQ1098742

EAST
♠ 53
♡ QJ9
◇ K10863
♣ J65

SOUTH
♠ AQ76
♡ AK65
◇ Q9754
♣ —

SOUTH	WEST	NORTH	EAST
—	1♣	Pass	1◇
Double	4♣	4♡	5♣
5♡	Pass	Pass	Pass

The bad breaks doomed the contract. Declarer won the club lead, and played a diamond. It was not obvious that

East should play the king—he ducked. Declarer ruffed the club return in dummy, ruffed a diamond, played a trump to dummy, saw the break, and ducked a spade to West. West led a club, ruffed in the North hand while dummy shed the spade queen. Then: second high heart, spade ace, diamond ruff, spade ruff, diamond ruff.

North–South minus 50.

Board 9

Where you had to decide whether to play three notrump or four hearts with a solid heart suit, your counterpart chose hearts, and your teammates rose to the occasion.

```
                    NORTH
                    ♠ AQ64
                    ♡ 3
                    ◇ K87
                    ♣ KQ874
    WEST                            EAST
    ♠ J1092                         ♠ K53
    ♡ 9652                          ♡ 87
    ◇ AJ3                           ◇ Q1042
    ♣ 105                           ♣ AJ96
                    SOUTH
                    ♠ 87
                    ♡ AKQJ104
                    ◇ 965
                    ♣ 32
```

SOUTH	WEST	NORTH	EAST
—	—	1♣	Pass
1♡	Pass	1♠	Pass
4♡	Pass	Pass	Pass

West led the jack of spades, ducked all around, then found the killing shift to a diamond. Don't fail to congratulate him for his well reasoned play.

North–South minus 50.

Board 10

Where you had to find an entry–killing play in trumps to defeat six hearts, your teammates had a serious misunderstanding.

WEST	EAST
♠ —	♠ Q109
♡ A973	♡ KQJ85
◊ 54	◊ AKJ32
♣ KQJ10862	♣ —

WEST	EAST
—	1♡
2♣	2◊
3♡	5♡
5♠	6♣
Pass	Glurf!

East thought he was cue–bidding as a seven–try: West didn't. However, the final contract was acceptable, and unbeatable on the lie of the cards.

North–South minus 1370.

Board 11

Where you played three clubs in a four–four fit your counterpart chose a different rebid.

NORTH
- ♠ QJ85
- ♡ A32
- ◇ 106
- ♣ K974

WEST
- ♠ K9764
- ♡ 10
- ◇ QJ82
- ♣ A53

EAST
- ♠ 1032
- ♡ K87654
- ◇ A9
- ♣ 62

SOUTH
- ♠ A
- ♡ QJ9
- ◇ K7543
- ♣ QJ108

SOUTH	WEST	NORTH	EAST
1◇	Pass	1♠	Pass
1NT	Pass	Pass	Pass

West led the four(!) of spades to the blank ace. Declarer attacked clubs. West won and found the diamond shift. South won the second diamond, and lost a heart finesse—that gave South seven tricks, and the defense six.

North–South plus 90.

Board 12

Where you had to finesse early against jack–fourth of trumps to make four hearts, your teammates stole the deal.

NORTH
♠ J7
♡ 875
◇ Q1085
♣ AKQ10

WEST
♠ AKQ92
♡ 4
◇ 74
♣ 76532

EAST
♠ 1085
♡ J632
◇ A9632
♣ J

SOUTH
♠ 643
♡ AKQ109
◇ KJ
♣ 984

SOUTH	WEST	NORTH	EAST
—	2♠	Pass	4♠
Pass	Pass	Pass	

North led the club king, and shifted to a trump. Declarer won, ruffed a club, lost the jack of hearts to South, won the trump return. drew the last trump. and worked on clubs. Down two.

North–South plus 100.

Board 13

Where you had to decide whether or not to sell to three hearts, your teammate did not find the raise on a doubleton.

NORTH
♠ Q3
♡ 1042
◇ AQJ9
♣ AK86

WEST
♠ A10972
♡ Q5
◇ 8652
♣ 107

EAST
♠ 4
♡ KJ9863
◇ K7
♣ QJ93

SOUTH
♠ KJ865
♡ A7
◇ 1043
♣ 542

SOUTH	WEST	NORTH	EAST
—	—	1NT	2♡
2♠	Pass	Pass	Pass

The play went badly for South. West led the club ten, won in dummy. The spade queen went to the ace, and another club was won in dummy. Now declarer played a spade to the king, and saw the break. He lost a diamond finesse to East; East played two high clubs allowing West to discard two losing diamonds while South ruffed. Declarer was restricted to two clubs, one diamond, one heart, two high spades and one club ruff.

North–South minus 100.

Board 14

Where you had to lead from your ace–queen–jack to establish the setting trick in time against five hearts, your teammates tried a slightly shaded weak two–bid.

NORTH
♠ J743
♡ A632
♢ 753
♣ 42

WEST
♠ A10
♡ K8
♢ K642
♣ AKJ73

EAST
♠ 5
♡ QJ10974
♢ 1098
♣ Q65

SOUTH
♠ KQ9862
♡ 5
♢ AQJ
♣ 1098

SOUTH	WEST	NORTH	EAST
—	—	—	2♡
2♠	4♡	4♠	Pass
Pass	Double	Pass	Pass
Pass			

North–South minus 100.

☐   ☐   ☐

The experts turned out to be fallible. Were you?

Match Three

The One–Club Team

"YOU WOULDN'T BELIEVE THIS TEAM WE JUST LOST TO, " says your friend as you sit down to play against him in the seventh match of an eight–round Sectional Swiss (each of your teams is five and one). "First, one of them makes three notrump by taking four tricks with king–jack–ten–third opposite the ace–empty–fourth, playing the king and running the jack; naturally, our declarer finessed the other way. Then, the other one forgets he is using a big–club system, so he passes his partner out in one club—not an easy contract to reach with those methods!—and it turns out that's all you can make. After that deal, they decide they'd better go back to Standard. This somehow takes them only five seconds and one change on the convention card. Sure enough, on the next deal they again reach one club, this time normally, and again it's all that can be made."

Your friend's misfortunes bode well for your own chances in this event. The "one–club team" is miraculously now six and zero; they are playing the only other team that is five and one, a team you have already beaten. So, if you win this match (a one–imp margin is all you need) you get to play the clowns in the final round. Of course, there is one small problem. Your friend's team is the class of the event, while yours is the usual crew—competent, but unspectacular. You grit your mental teeth . . .

Systems will be no problem in this round. Your area is a hotbed of Bridge World Standard.

Board 1

North dealer
None vulnerable

NORTH
♠ 1065
♡ J
◇ AK874
♣ A732

SOUTH
♠ QJ9872
♡ Q65
◇ Q3
♣ K10

SOUTH	WEST	NORTH	EAST
—	—	1◇	Pass
1♠	Pass	2♠	Pass
3♠	Pass	4♠	Pass
Pass	Pass		

The play proceeds:

> *Heart **king**, jack, two, five.*
> *Spade three, five, **king**, two.*
> *Spade **ace**, seven, heart four, six.*
> *Spade four, **queen**, heart seven, spade ten.*
> *Spade **nine**, club eight, club two, heart three.*

Plan the play

```
                    NORTH
                    ♠ 1065
                    ♡ J
                    ◇ AK874
                    ♣ A732
    WEST                            EAST
    ♠ 3                             ♠ AK4
    ♡ AK74                          ♡ 109832
    ◇ 109652                        ◇ J
    ♣ QJ8                           ♣ 9654
                    SOUTH
                    ♠ QJ9872
                    ♡ Q65
                    ◇ Q3
                    ♣ K10
```

It is highly unlikely that East has five diamonds (West wouldn't have passed one spade), so you don't have to worry about playing diamonds early to squeeze West between hearts and clubs.

If West has five diamonds, you can squeeze him between the red suits. However, you can't afford to play for that, since far more often West will have started with something like,

♠ x   ♡ AKxxx   ◇ xx   ♣ Jxxxx.

where you need to keep dummy's club ace as a reentry to the established long diamond; yet, the red–suit squeeze requires that you cash the club ace early.

However, you can afford to take into account the possibility that West, along with five diamonds, holds the queen–jack of clubs. Indeed, if you decide not to go for the red–suit squeeze you might as well cash the club king (to get to see another of West's cards), then lead the next–to–last trump, intending to throw a club from dummy and go for diamonds. If West has the hand shown, he must reveal his club honors before you discard from dummy on the penultimate trump. This allows you to cash the club ten for your tenth trick. (You wouldn't have invited game without the ten of clubs, would you?)

Results

If you played ace–king of clubs, then trumps (squeezing West on the lie of the cards), or, better, club king and trumps, plus 420. If you played on diamonds, or if you played a trump without first cashing the king of clubs (you wouldn't, we trust, discard a diamond from dummy when West discarded the club jack—West will own you for life if you play like that), you score minus 50.

Board 2

RHO is the dealer
Your side vulnerable

DUMMY
♠ KQJ8
♡ KQ3
♢ AQ97
♣ K3

YOU
♠ A75
♡ 4
♢ 10865432
♣ 76

LHO	PARTNER	RHO	YOU
—	—	1♢	Pass
1♠	2NT[1]	4♠	Pass
Pass	Pass		

[1] Hearts and clubs

Partner leads the heart jack; declarer wins in his hand with the ace, and leads the spade three to dummy's jack; partner plays the deuce.

Plan your defense.

```
                    NORTH
                    ♠ 62
                    ♡ J109865
                    ◇ —
                    ♣ AJ1094
        WEST                          EAST
        ♠ 10943                       ♠ KQJ8
        ♡ A72                         ♡ KQ3
        ◇ KJ                          ◇ AQ97
        ♣ Q852                        ♣ K3
                    SOUTH
                    ♠ A75
                    ♡ 4
                    ◇ 10865432
                    ♣ 76
```

On the vulnerability, partner needs the ace of clubs (he has escaped with his life as it is). Even so, it will take a diamond ruff to defeat the control. Partner may not be void of diamonds, or, if he is, he may well have started with 1–6–0–6. Playing a diamond at once risks an overtrick (your heart ruff). Might it not be better to take your heart ruff first, then go for the questionable diamond ruff?

No! If you win the spade and return a club, how does partner know whether to give you a heart ruff or a club ruff? You should avoid giving partner that headache by winning the spade ace and returning a high diamond, signalling for hearts. This way, if partner is void of diamonds you will definitely beat the contract.

Results

If you won the spade ace and returned a high diamond, plus 100. If you won the spade ace and led a club, minus 450—partner guessed wrong (don't they always?). Worse yet, he blames it on you (don't they always?).

Board 3

With the opponents vulnerable, you deal and pass with,

♠ 1098   ♡ J8642   ◇ K5   ♣ 765

The bidding continues:

YOU	LHO	PARTNER	RHO
Pass	Pass	Pass	2NT[1]
Pass	4NT	Pass	Pass
Pass			

[1] Good 20 to bad 22

What is your opening lead?

```
                    NORTH
                    ♠ J654
                    ♡ K107
                    ◇ 74
                    ♣ 9432
WEST                                    EAST
♠ Q32                                   ♠ AK7
♡ Q5                                    ♡ A93
◇ Q10862                                ◇ AJ93
♣ AQ8                                   ♣ KJ10
                    SOUTH
                    ♠ 1098
                    ♡ J8642
                    ◇ K5
                    ♣ 765
```

When an invitational four notrump is passed out, the opponents have substantial extra values. Except for rare cases in which a key suit breaks unusually badly, it takes aggressive defense to create such a contract. Thus, if you can see any reasonable chance of success through an attacking lead, you should make it.

Here, it is reasonable to hope that the king of diamonds is an entry (that it is in a minor is a good sign), and that partner has the heart length and strength to allow your suit to set up. This is far from a wild hope. It is a good sign that the suit you are attacking is a major.

Results

If you led a heart, plus 200; otherwise, minus 660.

Board 4

LHO is the dealer
Both vulnerable

DUMMY
♠ 764
♡ 1085
◇ AJ
♣ KQ932

YOU
♠ K852
♡ KQ7
◇ 8743
♣ 76

LHO	PARTNER	RHO	YOU
1NT	Pass	3NT	Pass
Pass	Pass		

The play proceeds:

*Heart four, five, **queen**, two.*

Plan your defense.

```
                NORTH
                ♠ Q93
                ♡ A9643
                ◇ 9652
                ♣ 5
    WEST                        EAST
    ♠ AJ10                      ♠ 764
    ♡ J2                        ♡ 1085
    ◇ KQ10                      ◇ AJ
    ♣ AJ1084                    ♣ KQ932
                SOUTH
                ♠ K852
                ♡ KQ7
                ◇ 8743
                ♣ 76
```

It is possible that a spade shift is needed For example, declarer might hold something like,

♠ AJ10　♡ A32　◇ KQ10　♣ J1085,

in which case you must lead a spade at trick two (preferably the eight, to tell partner to shift back to hearts if he wins the trick). It declarer wins, the defense can later run spades; if declarer ducks, the defense can go back to hearts.

However, there are at least two things wrong with shifting to the spade. The winning defense will far more often be the simple one—run five hearts. And, if the spade shift is right declarer has made a mistake—he should have taken the first trick with the heart ace. Everyone makes mistakes, true, but you are playing against a competent team.

Results

If you continued hearts, plus 100; if not, minus 600.

Board 5

North dealer
North–South vulnerable

You, South, hold:

♠ K7   ♡ KQ965   ◇ 52   ♣ A543

SOUTH	WEST	NORTH	EAST
—	—	Pass	Pass
1♡	3♣[1]	Double[2]	Pass
?			

[1] Preemptive
[2] Negative

What call do you make?

```
                    NORTH
                    ♠ A1096
                    ♡ J8
                    ◊ A10984
                    ♣ 72
    WEST                            EAST
    ♠ 43                            ♠ QJ852
    ♡ 2                             ♡ A10743
    ◊ KJ73                          ◊ Q6
    ♣ KQJ1086                       ♣ 9
                    SOUTH
                    ♠ K7
                    ♡ KQ965
                    ◊ 52
                    ♣ A543
```

Nobody said bridge was going to be easy—some days are filled with excruciating decisions. Passing the double is far and away the best chance for a plus, but is the chance of beating three clubs good enough? Passing is often the best way to handle these unclear negative double situations at the three level. You have no decent bid: three hearts is a blind guess about the trump suit; three notrump you can be fairly sure won't make.

The fate of three clubs doubled may hinge on a random ten or nine. You must judge your risks against the IMP odds. Suppose three hearts will go down one, as good a guess as any. Then, if three clubs would also be down one, we lose 200 by bidding: 5 imps. If three clubs makes, we lose 370 (the 470 the opponents score, less the 100 we would lose anyway at three hearts) by passing: 9 imps.

If it is at least two–to–one that three clubs doubled will go down (and we think it is), the risk of passing is worth taking. (Note, too, that in a short match a 5–imp swing will be decisive rather more than 5/9 as often as a 9–imp swing. The shorter a match, the more mathematically advantageous it is to go for the plus at the risk of a big minus.)

Results

If you passed, plus 100 (whew!), if you bid three hearts, minus 100: it you bid three notrump, minus 200.

Board 6

East dealer
East–West vulnerable

♠ J87   ♡ 1042   ◇ KQ9   ♣ A653

SOUTH	WEST	NORTH	EAST
—	—	—	Pass
Pass	4 ♡	4 ♠	Pass
?			

What call do you make?

```
              NORTH
              ♠ AK109654
              ♡ —
              ◇ A2
              ♣ K1087
WEST                          EAST
♠ —                           ♠ Q32
♡ AKQJ9875                    ♡ 63
◇ 1063                        ◇ J8754
♣ 42                          ♣ QJ9
              SOUTH
              ♠ J87
              ♡ 1042
              ◇ KQ9
              ♣ A653
```

You could easily have a good slam, even a laydown slam
(for example, if partner has a spade–diamond two– suiter).
Nonetheless, we believe it is best in the long run to give
partner leeway in these situations.

Good tactics require partner to push in on many
doubtful hands that are short in hearts and long in
spades. It may be necessary to bid spades to get your
side into the auction, perhaps for a make, perhaps for a
sacrifice (West's third–position opening at unfavorable
vulnerability may be based on quite a good hand), perhaps
to avoid a double–game swing. It is true that partner
may be unable to bid more than four spades with a huge
hand; there is no absolute answer to this problem. But
he may be counting on you not to be slam minded
because you passed originally. Really, the only special
feature of your hand is that you have no waste in hearts,
something partner may already have bid for.

Trying for slam has many risks. Even if partner has a
good hand he may be unable to bid six—then, you gain
nothing for the risk going down at five. And if partner

does bid six spades, as he would with his actual hand, you may find you have reached a contract that would normally be fine, but is only so–so after West opens four hearts. Going down at six spades with this North–South combination is not entirely bad luck.

Results

If you passed, plus 450; if not, minus 50.

Board 7

South dealer
Both vulnerable

NORTH
♠ A8
♡ Q1082
♢ Q10
♣ Q652

SOUTH
♠ —
♡ AKJ95
♢ AJ84
♣ AK107

SOUTH	WEST	NORTH	EAST
1♡	Pass	3♡	4♠
5♠	Pass	6♡	Double
Pass	Pass	Pass	

The play proceeds:

Club four, two, **heart four**, seven.
Diamond two, ?

Your move.

70

NORTH
♠ A8
♡ Q10872
◇ Q10
♣ Q652

WEST
♠ 652
♡ 3
◇ K963
♣ J9843

EAST
♠ KQJ109743
♡ 64
◇ 752
♣ —

SOUTH
♠ —
♡ AKJ95
◇ AJ84
♣ AK107

It's not easy to give up on making a doubled slam. but that is the course we recommend here. Taking the diamond finesse risks the loss of a second ruff, 300 points, a potential 7 imps (assuming the situation is roughly the same as in the other room). Refusing the finesse risks the value of the slam plus the penalty, a total of 1860, 18 imps (maybe even 27 imps, if they stop at game or double a spade sacrifice at the other table). A swing this size will almost certainly decide the match, even with these lively boards. However, 7 to 18 is not like the value of an overtrick to that of a game or slam; 7 imps is a substantial swing. Therefore, you cannot choose your play without looking at the technical issues involved.

This diamond finesse is not fifty–fifty. It's not clear whether East is more likely to bid and double (especially in the face of a grand–slam try!) with the king or without it, but there are two indications from the opponents' play. First, there is West's opening lead of a fairly low club—with a topless diamond suit, might he not have led a higher club to warn partner away from diamonds? Second, and far more significant, if East has the king of diamonds why has he taken the risk of shifting to that suit at trick two? He has no way of knowing you have the jack of diamonds. If he took that chance, he deserves to win. We think West has the king of diamonds, and we'd play to save the extra 300, hoping that the contract will be the same in the other room.

Results

If you finessed in diamonds, minus 500; if not, minus 200.

Post–Mortem

Board 1

Where you had a choice of extra squeeze chances at four spades, competition had the unusual effect of slowing down the bidding in the other room.

NORTH
♠ 1065
♡ J
♢ AK874
♣ A732

WEST
♠ 3
♡ AK74
♢ 109652
♣ QJ8

EAST
♠ AK4
♡ 109832
♢ J
♣ 9654

SOUTH
♠ QJ9872
♡ Q65
♢ Q3
♣ K10

SOUTH	WEST	NORTH	EAST
—	—	1♢	Pass
1♠	Double	2♠	3♡
3♠	Pass	Pass	Pass

Here, South's three spades was only a competitive effort, so North chose not to take the push with his weak trumps. The play started as in the other room: heart king, three rounds of trumps, another trump. Considering the bidding, declarer decided to start diamonds early to preserve the chance of a heart–club squeeze against West. Thus, he played four rounds of diamonds, then spades. However, East's nine of clubs proved a stopper, so declarer made only nine tricks.

(Do you think South would have changed his mind if he had played the club king first?)

North–South plus 140.

Board 2

Where you had to give partner an immediate ruff to make sure you got the correct ruff yourself, your teammates bid rather more effectively:

WEST	EAST
♠ KQJ8	♠ 10943
♡ KQ3	♡ A72
◊ AQ97	◊ KJ
♣ K3	♣ Q852

OPENER	RESPONDER
2NT	3NT
Pass	

Opener thought he had a "good" 20 (poor intermediates, but no disconnected lower honors); responder decided not to investigate for a four–four fit, with his extra strength and weak major.

A club lead would have held declarer to ten tricks, but the actual result was North–South minus 460.

Board 3

Where you had to make an aggressive lead to defeat four notrump, your teammate with the queeny twelve–count plus a five–card suit raised to six notrump. This was a sensible contract—finesses sometimes win—but was due to fail. Opening leader tried the passive spade ten from the hand you held,

♠ 1098   ♡ J8642   ◇ K5   ♣ 765,

and the result was down only one. Six notrump turned out to be safer than four notrump.

North–South plus 100.

Board 4

Where you had to return partner's suit to defeat three notrump (sounds easy when phrased like that, doesn't it?), the bidding was the same in the other room. Your counterparts were using "lowest to encourage" against notrump, so the opening lead was the three of hearts from A–9–6–4–3, making it a bit easier for their player to find the winning defense.

North–South plus 100.

Board 5

Where you had to decide whether or not to pass partner's three–level negative double with an all–around bad hand, there was no jump overcall in the other room.

                    NORTH
                    ♠ A1096
                    ♡ J8
                    ◇ A10984
                    ♣ 72

WEST   EAST
♠ 43   ♠ QJ852
♡ 2   ♡ A10743
◇ KJ73   ◇ Q6
♣ KQJ1086   ♣ 9

                    SOUTH
                    ♠ K7
                    ♡ KQ965
                    ◇ 52
                    ♣ A543

SOUTH	WEST	NORTH	EAST
—	—	Pass	Pass
1♡	2♣	Double	Pass
2♡	Pass	3♡	Pass
Pass	Pass		

North inferred that South had a decent hand since with a six–card heart suit he had not opened a weak two–bid. Some inferences turn out to be less reliable than others.

North–South minus 100.

Board 6

Your teammate tried an experiment with his solid eight–card suit.

```
              NORTH
              ♠ AK109654
              ♡ —
              ◊ A2
              ♣ K1087
WEST                        EAST
♠ —                         ♠ Q32
♡ AKQJ9875                  ♡ 63
◊ 1063                      ◊ J8754
♣ 42                        ♣ QJ9
              SOUTH
              ♠ J87
              ♡ 1042
              ◊ KQ9
              ♣ A653
```

SOUTH	WEST	NORTH	EAST
—	—	—	Pass
Pass	Pass!	1♠	Pass
1NT	Pass!!	3♠	Pass
4♠	Pass	Pass	Pass

Unfortunately, North–South missed the good slam.

Whom do you blame for this?

It is hard to locate the very good fit. North was slightly
conservative with his rebid, but, to be fair, his is a hard
hand to bid. South, however, clearly underbid. We agree
with his decision not to bid two clubs (strength plus fit)
after the fourth–position opening, since the hand is
relatively colorless. While we prefer a raise to two spades,
his one notrump was reasonable. However, having made
this decision he should surely have cue–bid over three
spades, since slam was possible.

North–South plus 450.

Board 7

Where you had an excruciating decision whether to give up all hope for a doubled slam by refusing a finesse, a bold move led to a different sort of play problem at the other table.

NORTH
♠ A8
♡ Q10872
♢ Q10
♣ Q652

WEST
♠ 652
♡ 3
♢ K963
♣ J9843

EAST
♠ KQJ109743
♡ 64
♢ 752
♣ —

SOUTH
♠ —
♡ AKJ95
♢ AJ84
♣ AK107

SOUTH	WEST	NORTH	EAST
1♡	Pass	3♡	4♠
5♠	Pass	6♡	Double
Pass	Pass	6NT	Pass
Pass	Double	Pass	Pass
Pass			

Declarer was in no doubt whatever about the location of the diamond king. He ducked the opening, spade lead (do you see why?), won the second spade and ran five hearts. Blanking the king of diamonds wouldn't have fooled anyone—declarer would not have played East for only seven spades for his bid. So West came down to four clubs and two diamonds. Declarer then played four rounds of clubs to endplay West.

North–South minus 200.

☐   ☐   ☐

Will you get your shot at the "one–club team"?

Match Four

One Football Sunday

YOU HAVE GIVEN UP A FALL FOOTBALL SUNDAY to play in a sectional Swiss; you are determined to make the most of it, and fancy your chances. Your teammates have never made it to the last sixteen in a national knockout, but they are one of the class pairs in this event. They are well practiced, and approach the game in a straightforward fashion, nothing tricky. Your partner is an old–timer, a reformed Roth–Stoner who has agreed to use Bridge World Standard in the interests of team solidarity. However, he insists on a few things to make him feel more comfortable: weak preempts, weak jump overcalls, weak jump responses, weak jump raises of overcalls, weak two–suited cue–bids, weak two–bids . . . if his methods were any weaker they'd be limp.

Scoring is win–loss: an exact imp tie is required for a draw. There are eight seven–board matches, and the field is not huge, so 7–1 might win. Your first match, which you win easily against a group of locals out for exercise, is not too interesting. Your second match, against a team of greater capability, would have been close if your opponents had not bid a foolish slam.

In the third match, you face slightly familiar opponents. Your right–hand opponent is a sound player (a Bridge World subscriber), but not an expert. Your left– hand opponent is flaky, but you have seen him make the "Big Play" on occasion. Their teammates are sound, though not as good as yours. This team can beat you with some luck, or if your side is below form.

Board 1

North dealer
None vulnerable

NORTH
♠ 7
♡ AK87
◇ A52
♣ AK652

SOUTH
♠ Q104
♡ Q76532
◇ 104
♣ 73

SOUTH	WEST	NORTH	EAST
—	—	1♣	Pass
2♡[1]	Pass	6♡	Pass
Pass[2]	Pass		

[1] Weak—you remembered!
[2] You hope *he* did.

Six hearts is a good contract, especially after bidding that gives little clue to the most effective opening lead. After a spade lead, which establishes declarer's transportation, chances are excellent. Unfortunately, *West leads the king of diamonds.*

Plan the play.

NORTH
- ♠ 7
- ♡ AK87
- ◊ A52
- ♣ AK652

WEST
- ♠ A652
- ♡ J
- ◊ KQ73
- ♣ 10984

EAST
- ♠ KJ983
- ♡ 109
- ◊ J986
- ♣ QJ

SOUTH
- ♠ Q104
- ♡ Q76532
- ◊ 104
- ♣ 73

You need a discard from clubs before losing the lead. Also, if clubs are four–two you need to ruff two spades in dummy. Therefore, drawing trumps (or even playing one high one) is tantamount to depending on a three–three club break, since this kills a quick reentry to dummy.

It's better to win the ace of diamonds, then play ace, king and another club right away. If East follows to the third club, ruff queen and hope for the best. (Ruffing with the queen gains if East started with four clubs and two hearts, since the play continues: heart to the ace, extracting West's only trump: club ruff low; heart to the king; club pitching a diamond; spade. Ruffing with the queen loses if clubs are three–three and trumps three–zero, which is slightly less likely.)

The advantage to this approach appears when East shows out on the third club. If he ruffs, you overruff, play a trump to dummy and continue clubs; all is well if East started with one or two trumps. If East discards, you can ruff low and proceed in relative comfort. In effect, this line adds the possibility of East's holding exactly two clubs to your other chances.

Results

On the lie of the cards, if you play correctly, leading clubs at tricks two, three and four, you make the contract—plus 980. Delaying the club play dooms the slam—minus 50.

Board 2

East dealer
North–South vulnerable

You, South, hold

♠ AKQ62   ♡ AQ3   ◇ A6   ♣ 642

SOUTH	WEST	NORTH	EAST
—	—	—	Pass
1♠	Pass	2◇	Pass
?			

What call do you make?

```
                    NORTH
                    ♠ 83
                    ♡ KJ108
                    ◇ KQ873
                    ♣ K5
      WEST                          EAST
      ♠ 109754                      ♠ J
      ♡ 5                           ♡ 97642
      ◇ 104                         ◇ J952
      ♣ Q10873                      ♣ AJ9
                    SOUTH
                    ♠ AKQ62
                    ♡ AQ3
                    ◇ A6
                    ♣ 642
```

If there is a "right" rebid with the South cards, we don't know what it is: we can't even find anyone who claims to know. We suspect that two hearts would be popular in the expert community, especially when the expert questioned doesn't have to worry about the rest of the auction.

Many experts would bid two spades, hoping to be able to make a sensible limit bid later on (e.g., raise two notrump to four notrump). This is a technically correct action, though perhaps risky with a new partner.

It's a little easier to judge where you'd like to end up (looking only at the North–South cards). Six hearts by North looks best—it will make over 70% of the time. However, six notrump by North, which is a favorite, and is greatly improved on a club lead, is not far behind.

Results

Action	Final Contract	Result
2♡ or 3♡	6NT(N)	−100
2♠	4NT(N)	+660
2NT	4NT(S)	−200
3♣ or 3♠	3NT(N)	+600
3NT	3NT(S)	−100

Board 3

You are the dealer
Opponents vulnerable

DUMMY
♠ 2
♡ Q95
◇ K10
♣ AK87642

YOU
♠ 865
♡ AK1073
◇ AQJ6
♣ Q

YOU	LHO	PARTNER	RHO
1♡	2♣	Pass	4♠
Pass	Pass	Pass	

You lead the heart king: five, deuce, six.

What now?

```
                    NORTH
                    ♠ 943
                    ♡ J842
                    ◇ 753
                    ♣ J109
    WEST                            EAST
    ♠ 2                             ♠ AKQJ107
    ♡ Q95                           ♡ 6
    ◇ K10                           ◇ 9842
    ♣ AK87642                       ♣ 53
                    SOUTH
                    ♠ 865
                    ♡ AK1073
                    ◇ AQJ6
                    ♣ Q
```

One possible hope to defeat the contract is that partner's
heart was a singleton. If this were the situation, it would
probably be fatal not to continue hearts.

However, that is an unlikely setup. RHO (East) might
have tried for three notrump with four hearts to the jack
and long, solid spades—he must have solid spades, since
there are no other significant honors unaccounted for.

Assuming East does not have four hearts, shifting to the
six of diamonds will defeat the contract virtually whenever
it can be defeated. If declarer has seven solid spades there
is no hope. If he has only six solid spades, he has nine tricks:
six spades, one diamond, two clubs; given time, he can
establish clubs, with a ruff or an unblock, and reach them
with the king of diamonds. Alternatively, if declarer started
with a singleton club, he can lead towards the queen of
hearts for his tenth trick. A diamond shift kills the entry,
and sets up South's winners; declarer cannot ruff a
diamond in dummy (if he wins and continues diamonds,
you lead a trump). If declarer wins the diamond shift in
dummy and leads a heart to his (hypothetical) doubleton

jack (he can't afford to pull trumps, which would bare his diamond losers), you win and shift to a club, still defeating the contract when East started with 6–2–4–1 distribution (declarer can take only six spades, one heart, one diamond and one club).

Results

If you shift to the diamond six, plus 100. If you shift to ace and another diamond, or to the diamond queen or jack, or to a club, minus 620. If you shift to a trump, or play another heart, minus 650.

Board 4

West dealer
Both vulnerable

NORTH
♠ 84
♡ KQ7
♢ 10963
♣ A52

SOUTH
♠ AQ
♡ AJ10
♢ Q54
♣ K10873

SOUTH	WEST	NORTH	EAST
1NT	Pass	3NT	Pass
Pass	Pass		

West leads the spade five: four, king, ace.

How do you proceed?

```
                    NORTH
                    ♠ 84
                    ♡ KQ7
                    ◇ J10963
                    ♣ A52
        WEST                        EAST
        ♠ J975                      ♠ K10632
        ♡ 9653                      ♡ 842
        ◇ K872                      ◇ A
        ♣ Q                         ♣ J964
                    SOUTH
                    ♠ AQ
                    ♡ AJ10
                    ◇ Q54
                    ♣ K10873
```

There is not time to go for diamonds, so you need four tricks from clubs. All three–two breaks make it easy: both five–zero breaks make it impossible. What about the four–ones? You're a sure loser if East has singleton six or four. So, your objective is to play clubs in such a way as to lose to the fewest of the other eight singletons.

Leading and running the seven is a weak attempt. It loses when East has singleton queen, jack or nine, and when West has singleton six or four. Leading the ten is a little better, since it picks up East's singleton nine. Cashing the ace of clubs first is better yet, losing only when East has singleton queen, jack or nine. It is no better to cash the king first: you lose to West's singleton nine, six or four. If you lead towards the king, intending to finesse the ten, you lose only to West's singleton queen or jack. If you lead towards the king, intending to finesse the seven you necessarily lose only to West's singleton nine—best! So, you should play a heart to dummy at trick two, then a low club. If East plays an honor, win the king and lead the seven, intending to run it: if East, instead, follows low, finesse the seven.

An interesting speculation is what declarer should do if East plays the nine on the first round of clubs. Assuming that East will defend perfectly, declarer's best play is to finesse the ten. If this loses, declarer cannot afford (on any normal basis) to finesse on the next round of the suit, so he will lose to singleton nine *in either hand*. However, most human defenders don't play the nine from queen–jack–nine–small, even if they should.

Take credit for a semester of mathematics (but no extra imps) if you worked all that out.

Results

If you cashed the ace or led the 8, 7 or 3 towards the ace, plus 630. If you cashed the king, or led the ten, or led to the seven, plus 600. If you lead to the ten, minus 200.

Board 5

North dealer
North–South vulnerable

You, South, hold:

♠ 1043   ♡ KQJ642   ◇ None   ♣ K1093

SOUTH	WEST	NORTH	EAST
—	—	Pass	1♠
?			

What call do you make?

There is nothing safe about an overcall of two hearts. However, it is even more dangerous to pass, perhaps keeping your side out of the auction completely. It is fallacious to suppose that just because any action is fraught with risk pass must be safest. To overcall here is a risk that has to be taken, results aside.

You overcall two hearts. The bidding continues.

SOUTH	WEST	NORTH	EAST
—	—	Pass	1♠
2♡	Double[1]	2♠	4♠
Pass	Pass	Double	Pass
Pass	Pass		

[1] Negative double

What is your opening lead?

The main issue is whether you should make a lead that suggests your diamond void. We have no strong feelings about this—it might be good, it might be bad. However, if you want to make a "special" lead, it should be the jack of hearts rather than the deuce.

The deuce–lead is slightly risky in the suit itself (declarer might profitably win a trick with the ten of hearts). Furthermore, it tells declarer as well as partner about your void suit: the jack–lead might tell partner without telling declarer. North is far more likely to have the secret–revealing ten of hearts than East: even if East has it, he may be forced to show it immediately (a singleton), or early in the play. Note that if declarer cannot see the ten of hearts, he will presume that the lead is normal, from a suit head by king–jack–ten.

```
                    NORTH
                    ♠ Q95
                    ♡ A1087
                    ◇ 8752
                    ♣ AJ
    WEST                            EAST
    ♠ J                             ♠ AK8762
    ♡ —                             ♡ 953
    ◇ K109643                       ◇ AQJ
    ♣ Q87654                        ♣ 2
                    SOUTH
                    ♠ 1043
                    ♡ KQJ642
                    ◇ —
                    ♣ K1093
```

Not everybody's negative double!

Results

If you passed one spade, minus 80. Otherwise: If, against four spades doubled, you remarkably led a club, plus 100. If you led a trump, plus 300. If you led the king of hearts or jack of hearts, plus 800 (declarer's choice at trick two is close; not tipped off by your opening lead, he guessed wrong). If you lead the two of hearts, plus 500. (Theorists may enjoy determining how to solve the signaling problem that arises after: opening heart lead ruffed, club to the ace, eight of diamonds ruffed? Interesting things also happen if declarer decides to discard from dummy on the opening lead. We leave this to you.)

Board 6

East dealer
East–West vulnerable

You, South, hold:

♠ A9   ♡ 3   ◇ KQJ872   ♣ AQ63

The bidding proceeds:

SOUTH	WEST	NORTH	EAST
—	—	—	Pass
1◇	Pass	1♡	Pass
?			

What is your rebid?

The hand is far too good for a simple two diamonds, so the choice is between three diamonds and two clubs. Two clubs leaves you more opportunity to describe your complicated hand, while three diamonds places too much emphasis on three notrump. The danger of two clubs is that partner will pass when there is a game. Still, if partner has any decent values at all he will give you false preference to diamonds with a doubleton (remember his background). And if he passes with a singleton diamond, unless it's the ace or ten you are unlikely to have missed much.

You rebid two clubs and partner raises to three clubs.

What now?

Both three diamonds and three spades are acceptable choices. Three diamonds is descriptive, but an ex–Roth–Stoner will then consider your club suit suspect—and really it isn't. Three spades also hints at slam possibilities, which certainly matches your playing strength and controls.

You try three spades. Partner bids four diamonds.

What call do you make? What rebid do you plan over partner's likely action?

Partner, by bidding above the level of four clubs, has made an encouraging noise; and he was not interested in three notrump—he doesn't have too much in hearts. Very likely he has the ace of diamonds, king of clubs, and either another big card or some potentially useful bits (e.g. king of spades, or queen of spades plus jack of clubs). In any case, you already know that six clubs is an acceptable contract, depending at worst on decent splits in the minors. So, you should plan to drive to slam.

But to which slam? If partner cannot control the second round of spades, you will want to play in clubs to get an extra trick from the four–four fit, discarding his spades on your diamonds and ruffing a spade in his hand. However. if he does have second–round control of spades, the hand will almost certainly belong in diamonds, the solid suit, for fear of a fourth–round club loser. In diamonds, a four–one club break might be overcome by a finesse of the jack of spades, or something interesting happening in hearts, or a squeeze, or perhaps a mistake. None of these, not even the mistake, will happen if the opponents' tricks are the heart ace plus a sure trump trick.

Accordingly, your plan should be to cue–bid four hearts, with the intention of bidding six diamonds if partner cue–bids four spades, six clubs if he does not.

NORTH
♠ K105
♡ J974
♢ A4
♣ K752

WEST
♠ Q74
♡ AK862
♢ 1095
♣ J

EAST
♠ J862
♡ Q105
♢ 63
♣ 10984

SOUTH
♠ A9
♡ 3
♢ KQJ872
♣ AQ63

Certainly you will do well if you never reach a worse contract than six clubs. But six diamonds is better, and this time the cards don't forgive.

Six diamonds offers some interesting double–dummy possibilities, but in practice it will be made. For example, if West leads the king of hearts, and then finds the pretty shift to the queen of spades, declarer is in control. (Ace of spades, king of diamonds, ace of diamonds heart ruff, draw the last trump throwing a club from dummy, ace of clubs, king of clubs, heart ruff; now, declarer will usually have enough information to proceed successfully. In this case, a high club and the last trump effect a double squeeze; South doesn't care where the jack of spades is.)

Results

If your last bid was five clubs, plus 400; if five diamonds, plus 420; if six clubs, minus 50; if six diamonds, plus 920.

Board 7

You are the dealer
Both vulnerable

DUMMY (RHO)
♠ A87
♡ J10
♢ QJ832
♣ J96

YOU
♠ 65
♡ Q9743
♢ K64
♣ 532

LHO	PARTNER	RHO	YOU
—	—	—	Pass
1♣	2♣[1]	3♣	3♡
5♣	Pass	Pass	Pass

[1] "Weak" (less than old–fashioned Roth–Stone opening bid values) two–suiter in the majors

Partner leads the queen of spades. Declarer thinks for more than a few seconds, then wins dummy's ace of spades (following with the deuce from the closed hand), he leads the queen of diamonds from dummy.

Your move.

```
                    NORTH
                  ♠ QJ943
                  ♡ K8652
                  ◇ A107
                  ♣ —
    WEST                              EAST
  ♠ K102                            ♠ A87
  ♡ A                               ♡ J10
  ◇ 95                              ◇ QJ832
  ♣ AKQ10874                        ♣ J96
                    SOUTH
                  ♠ 65
                  ♡ Q9743
                  ◇ K64
                  ♣ 532
```

Partner needs a minor–suit ace for the contract to be breakable. If he has the ace of clubs, your play in diamonds is unlikely to matter. Declarer will almost certainly guess right in diamonds if he is missing the ten.

However, if partner's ace is in diamonds (more likely, anyway), you may need to get in early with your king of diamonds, to set up a defensive spade trick before partner's entry is driven out. The actual diagram is typical, and covering with the king of diamonds is unlikely to cost anything. Note declarer's cute play in diamonds—it would be easier for you win the first defensive diamond trick if he led diamonds from the closed hand, and also if the first lead from dummy were low. The three trump entries to dummy allowed him the luxury.

Results

If you play your king of diamonds and return a spade, you earn plus 100: otherwise you earn minus 600.

Post–Mortem

Board 1

Where you played six hearts with queen–sixth opposite ace–king–fourth, the bidding at your teammates' table was:

SOUTH	WEST	NORTH	EAST
—	—	1 ♣	Pass
Pass	1 ♠	Double	2 ♠
3 ♡	Pass	4 ♡	Pass
Pass	Pass		

Declarer made 11 tricks, for North–South plus 450.

West, who faced a difficult problem, keeps mumbling that he could have passed out the opponents, cold for slam, in one club. East has quite a lot to say about what might have happened at four spades doubled, after three rounds of clubs.

Board 2

North began by misarranging one of his diamonds into his hearts, which led to this sequence:

SOUTH	WEST	NORTH	EAST
—	—	—	Pass
1♠	Pass	2♡	Pass
3♢	Pass	4♢	Pass
4♠	Pass	6♢	Pass
6♡	Pass	Pass	Pass

NORTH
♠ 83
♡ KJ108
♢ KQ873
♣ K5

WEST
♠ 109754
♡ 5
♢ 104
♣ Q10873

EAST
♠ J
♡ 97642
♢ J952
♣ AJ9

SOUTH
♠ AKQ62
♡ AQ3
♢ A6
♣ 642

See, there's always some way to get to the right contract! Declarer, North, after almost attempting to win the trump opening lead with the seven of diamonds, rearranged his hand, won instead with the eight of hearts, looked over the dummy, smiled, played ace–king–small of diamonds ruffing with the ace, led queen of hearts from dummy—and then said some very bad words. Easy come, easy go. North–South minus 100.

Board 3

NORTH
♠ 943
♡ J842
◇ 753
♣ J109

WEST
♠ 2
♡ Q95
◇ K10
♣ AK87642

EAST
♠ AKQJ107
♡ 6
◇ 9842
♣ 53

SOUTH
♠ 865
♡ AK1073
◇ AQJ6
♣ Q

Your teammate, East, after the same early auction, made a conservative jump to three spades (invitational). All passed; the defender with your cards led king of hearts, saw the same first trick you did, then led the ace of hearts. North–South minus 200. Was that defense sensible or stupid?

It was sensible. The best chance for five tricks on defense is four hearts and a diamond, which can happen only when declarer has four hearts: heart, heart, heart ruff, diamond, heart overruff. It would not always cost two overtricks to play the ace of hearts at trick two.

While you are working that out, your teammates are discussing whether they belong in three notrump, and if so how to get there.

Board 4

Where you had to play ♣A52 opposite ♣K10873 for four tricks, with no strong clue as to which opponent was more likely to hold a singleton, your opposite number gave the matter hardly a second's thought. At trick two, he led to dummy's ace of clubs, gobbling up West's queen, then played a club to his seven (note an uncommon application of restricted choice here), for North–South plus 630.

Does that make you feel bad? It shouldn't. Think what would have happened, and how you would have felt. if you had played correctly, he had played his way, and West's singleton had been the nine.

Board 5

NORTH
♠ Q95
♡ A1087
◇ 8752
♣ AJ

WEST
♠ J
♡ —
◇ K109643
♣ Q87654

EAST
♠ AK8762
♡ 953
◇ AQJ
♣ 2

SOUTH
♠ 1043
♡ KQJ642
◇ —
♣ K1093

The bidding at the other table was:

SOUTH	WEST	NORTH	EAST
—	—	Pass	1 ♠
2 ♡	Pass	4 ♡	Pass
Pass	4NT	Double	Pass
5 ♡	Pass	Pass	Pass

West led the jack of spades, and East played three rounds. Declarer won the third round with the ten while West pitched two diamonds. South, misled by East's reluctance to name a minor, and perhaps also by West's diamond discards, decided to avoid guessing the location of the queen of clubs when East had 6–3–2–2. He played one high trump from the closed hand, then ace and another club, intending to ruff two clubs high in dummy and finesse in trumps. However, East ruffed the second club. North–South minus 100.

Can you see where declarer went wrong?

South first went wrong in the bidding. If he intended to insist on five hearts (itself questionable), he would have had more clues for the play had he arrived there more slowly.

But where South went disastrously wrong was in the play. He should have played the ten of spades from the closed hand at trick two, to win trick three in dummy *and ruff a diamond.* Then, a heart to the ace and another diamond ruff. When East follows twice in diamonds, he can't have as many as three clubs; declarer has a sure thing by drawing trumps, and taking a ruffing finesse against West (similarly if East throws a club on the second diamond). If East throws a spade on the second diamond, he still holds three clubs, so declarer can safely ruff a club low (and later ruff one high). Declarer had a certainty with careful play.

Even after failing to unblock in spades, declarer still could have tried the discovery play by ruffing diamonds, using on trump and the ace of clubs as entries. This would lose only when East was void of clubs, whereas the actual line loses also when East has a singleton club.

Board 6

NORTH
♠ K105
♡ J974
◇ A4
♣ K752

WEST
♠ Q74
♡ AK862
◇ 1095
♣ J

EAST
♠ J862
♡ Q105
◇ 63
♣ 10984

SOUTH
♠ A9
♡ 3
◇ KQJ872
♣ AQ63

Where your two club rebid led you to a slam decision and a choice between minors, the players in your seats bid:

SOUTH	WEST	NORTH	EAST
—	—	—	Pass
1◇	Pass	1♡	Pass
3◇	Pass	3NT	Pass
Pass	Pass		

They scored 460 North–South, after a spade lead from East.

Board 7

NORTH
♠ QJ943
♡ K8652
♢ A107
♣ —

WEST
♠ K102
♡ A
♢ 95
♣ AKQ10874

EAST
♠ A87
♡ J10
♢ QJ832
♣ J96

SOUTH
♠ 65
♡ Q9743
♢ K64
♣ 532

Your teammates underbid:

SOUTH	WEST	NORTH	EAST
Pass	1♣	Double	Pass
1♡	3♣	Pass	Pass
Pass			

North led a heart, and North–South were minus 150.

This time (compare with Board 3), your teammates know they should have been in three notrump, and they get into a wrangle about how the bidding should have gone. Of course, had they bid three notrump North–South might have bid four hearts. East–West can bid four notrump, but if they choose to defend four hearts they would probably regret it mightily, a double–game–swing's worth, because to beat it West has to lead a diamond (fat chance!), and later play the king of spades on the first round of the suit (that part

105

is easy, looking at North's hand in the dummy). In fact, if North were the declarer at four hearts, to beat it East would have to lead the queen of diamonds, and West would have put up the king of spades when the suit was led from dummy (South), a delightful symmetry when compared with the events in the other room.

☐   ☐   ☐

While your teammates continue their "discussion," you add up the scores and submit the result. How did you do?

Match Five

Visiting Firemen

AS A SPECIAL EVENT, your club has arranged a Club Championship in the form of a two–session Swiss teams, to be played on consecutive weekday evenings. The first night, four matches are scored by win–loss (but you have to win by more than 3 imps for a victory; a win by 1, 2 or 3 counts as a tie, a half–point to each team), with half the field qualifying for a four–match final the next night. Non–qualifiers get to play in a new one–session Swiss (or stay home if they prefer) the second night. It sounds like fun, so you enter with your usual team: a partner who plays with great care but little imagination (not such a bad combination for team play), and teammates who play with great imagination but, alas, random care.

Much to everyone's surprise, who should turn up but a team of nationally known experts, most of whom live all the way on the other side of the county? They rarely play in local events, and never at your club. Obviously, they are practicing for something to do with the National tournament coming up in less than a month. You'd like to have a chance to play against them, but attendance is surprisingly large. It looks as though you'll have to win the right to play the masters by getting a good score, and being drawn against them in a late round. However, your chance comes much sooner than you expect. You win your first seven–board match, 29–0, against a very weak team, and suddenly, in the second round, there you are! This is your chance to be a local hero.

Board 1

North dealer
None vulnerable

You, South, hold:

♠ K652   ♡ 53   ◇ 10862   ♣ Q105

SOUTH	WEST	NORTH	EAST
—	—	1♡	Double
Pass	2♣	2◇	3♣
?			

What call do you make?

NORTH
♠ J4
♡ AK862
◇ AQ743
♣ 2

WEST
♠ 973
♡ QJ1097
◇ 5
♣ J873

EAST
♠ AQ108
♡ 4
◇ KJ9
♣ AK964

SOUTH
♠ K652
♡ 53
◇ 10862
♣ Q105

Your hand presents conflicting values. You have substantial red–suit length on his auction, which suggests bidding. Yet, virtually all your honor strength is outside partner's suits, which suggests defending.

On the theoretical side, the imp–odds favor bidding, as they so often do: if you can beat them and can't make yourself, you lose in 50s; if you are wrong the other way, and everyone can make, you lose in 110s. (Also, if you "split" on the results you win 2 imps for bidding, 110 vs. 50.) As against that, when the strength is split fairly evenly, as it clearly is here, no one is a favorite to make a three–level contract.

We would resolve this particular dilemma by the nature or our values. The club values are clearly defensive, the red length clearly offensive. What about the king of spades? If that is purely a defensive card, the balance would swing to defense. However, it isn't—it is an offensive king as well. The opponents aren't likely to bid this way with eight spades (each of them had a convenient chance to mention the suit, but neither did).

So, partner probably has two spades, in which case the spade king will usually be a trick (and an entry) for him, since West is unlikely to have an ace. This swings the balance in favor of bidding.

Results

If you passed, minus 110. If you doubled, minus 470. If you bid three diamonds, plus 110. (Try switching the spade and club kings with the queens, and see what would happen.)

What is the correct play at three diamonds after the club–king lead and a heart shift?

Declarer should win, and play a spade towards the king. This will score the spade trick early (just in case East can effectively discard spades); and it develops declarer's transportation while hampering the defense's entries. If the spade king is allowed to win, declarer can continue with the club queen, discarding his last spade, to make sure that the defense cannot transfer the lead later on. Then, declarer goes about his business trying to ruff hearts.

Board 2

RHO is the dealer
Your side vulnerable

DUMMY (RHO)
♠ 5
♡ Q962
◇ A54
♣ J8743

YOU
♠ A964
♡ 87
◇ J97
♣ AQ96

YOU	LHO	PARTNER	RHO
—	—	—	Pass
Pass	1♠	Pass	1NT
Pass	2♡	Pass	3♡
Pass	4♡	Pass	Pass
Pass			

Partner leads the diamond eight. Declarer wins dummy's ace.

You must think fast! You know perfectly well what is going to be led to trick two. Just in case it is important to conceal your problem, you want to think now, while playing your diamond seven in normal tempo. Declarer follows, and here comes the singleton spade from dummy . . .

Play, right now!

```
                    NORTH
                    ♠ Q83
                    ♡ 1053
                    ◇ Q1082
                    ♣ K105
    WEST                            EAST
    ♠ KJ1072                        ♠ 5
    ♡ AKJ4                          ♡ Q962
    ◇ K63                           ◇ A54
    ♣ 2                             ♣ J8743
                    SOUTH
                    ♠ A964
                    ♡ 87
                    ◇ J97
                    ♣ AQ96
```

It is at best difficult (and perhaps impossible, but we aren't going to worry about that) to construct a deal consistent with the bidding on which it is essential to rise with the ace of spades. In fact, in general it is wrong to grab an ace when a lead is made towards declarer's long side suit. Taking the ace is indicated only when there is a pressing necessity to lead something im mediately (a trump, perhaps; or a lead through from the "right" side), or when you hope to cash out immediately to set the contract.

Neither of those exceptions comes anywhere near applying to this deal. You are in no rush to lead anything. And declarer doesn't have fast diamonds to lose. (Partner would not underlead king–queen, so declarer has at least one honor; if the queen, he would have ducked the first trick. So, declarer has the king, and partner the queen else a more aggressive club lead would likely have been preferred. Taking the lead into consideration, it is now certain declarer started with king–third in diamonds.)

Once you know you can't set the contract off the top, there can hardly be any need to rush in with your ace of spades. Its value won't be lost. Usually, you will break even at worst, and declarer may have to guess well for that. With king–queen–ten of spades declarer may finesse the ten, and with king–jack declarer may misguess, putting him a trick and at least one tempo behind where he was before. In the actual deal, declarer can make his contract if he guesses to put up the king of spades. But why should he? When he finesses the spade jack, as almost anyone would, partner can win and return a trump. See if you can do any good for declarer now; try double dummy if necessary. This illustrates why you must play both the first two tricks in normal tempo. (By the way, that is a good reason to be familiar with this common position in advance. You are going to duck unless, in the time available to you, you are able to spot that you are dealing with an exceptional case.)

Results

If you played the ace of spades, minus 420. If you took too long to duck the ace or spades, minus 420. If you took too long to play to the first trick, minus 420. (Declarer is not sleeping, remember.) If you are not sure whether or not you took too long, minus 420. Otherwise, plus 50.

Board 3

You are the dealer
Opponents vulnerable

DUMMY
♠ Q94
♡ 53
◇ 1032
♣ KJ1086

YOU
♠ K103
♡ Q984
◇ J76
♣ A52

YOU	LHO	PARTNER	RHO
Pass	2NT[1]	Pass	3NT
Pass	Pass	Pass	

[1] 20–21

Partner leads the spade deuce. Dummy plays the four.

Plan your defense.

```
              NORTH
              ♠ J762
              ♡ K107
              ◊ 9854
              ♣ 43
WEST                        EAST
♠ A85                       ♠ Q94
♡ AJ62                      ♡ 53
◊ AKQ                       ◊ 1032
♣ Q97                       ♣ KJ1086
              SOUTH
              ♠ K103
              ♡ Q984
              ◊ J76
              ♣ A52
```

The situation appears innocent enough, but the fate of the deal hinges on the card you play to trick one. If the ten, declarer can clear clubs, win the second round of hearts to block the suit, and force entry to dummy in spades by guessing right. All of that has to happen, true, but each of those plays for declarer is indicated. In contrast, if you play the three of spades to trick one, and the defense doesn't do something silly later on, declarer has only eight tricks no matter what approach he takes.

But how can you tell? In an absolute sense, you can't. However, consider partner's honor holding in spades. If declarer has his advertised twenty points, partner can't hold the ace–jack. When partner has the ace only, it doesn't matter whether you play the ten or the three. If partner has no spade honor, it can't help to play the ten but might hurt, by allowing declarer to get a needed entry, winning with the ace from ace–jack–third. Finally, what if partner has the jack? The advantage of playing the ten is that it may give declarer a guess later, but a guess he is likely to get right (the "percentage play" wins). A successful guess also gives him an entry.

Ducking deprives dummy of the late reentry. The actual layout is hardly the only possibility, but playing the spade three is much more likely to gain than lose.

Results

If you played the spade three, plus 100. If you played the spade ten, minus 600. If you played the spade king, minus 630.

Board 4

West dealer
Both vulnerable

> **NORTH**
> ♠ A643
> ♡ 7
> ◇ Q74
> ♣ AK652

> **SOUTH**
> ♠ K8
> ♡ AQJ1032
> ◇ 95
> ♣ 764

SOUTH	WEST	NORTH	EAST
—	3◇	Pass	Pass
3♡	Pass	4♣	Pass
4♡	Pass	Pass	Pass

West leads the diamond king, continues with the ace and the six. East follows with the diamond jack, discards the club three, then ruffs with the heart six.

Plan the play.

                    NORTH
                    ♠ A643
                    ♡ 7
                    ◊ Q74
                    ♣ AK652
WEST   EAST
♠ Q97   ♠ J1052
♡ 54   ♡ K986
◊ AK108632   ◊ J
♣ J   ♣ Q1093
                    SOUTH
                    ♠ K8
                    ♡ AQJ1032
                    ◊ 95
                    ♣ 764

Your basic plan should be to squeeze East in the black suits. However, your best chance to bring that squeeze about is to give up the trump finesse.

Let's see why. Suppose East started with four hearts to the king; not knowing that, you try to pick up his trumps by overruffing at trick three, entering dummy, and taking the heart finesse. If you enter dummy with the ace of spades, East, when he gets in with the king of hearts, will lead a club—bye–bye squeeze! It is better to use a club entry for the finesse; now, when East gets in with the king of hearts and returns a club, you can win in dummy, return the king of spades, and finish your trumps. This will squeeze East if West cannot guard the third round of spades. However, it will fail otherwise, as in the diagrammed deal.

The correct line is to give up the trump finesse, and play ace–queen of hearts after overruffing. When East plays a club (he can't do any better), you win in dummy, lead to the spade king, and play trumps until you reach this position:

NORTH

♠ A64
♡ —
♢ —
♣ A

SOUTH

♠ 8
♡ 2
♢ —
♣ 76

If the squeeze is available, East has already felt the pinch. You play a spade to dummy's ace. (If necessary—that is, if East did not exit with a club when he won the heart king—you clear away one of dummy's two club honors for better vision.) Then, you guess which black suit can now be run (even against the world's greatest, you will get it right most of the time).

This is far the best play. Suppose that East was originally dealt king–third of hearts, so that the trump finesse would have landed the contract. Giving up the finesse makes the contract except when West was dealt 0–3–7–3 (he guards clubs); but if West had that unlikely shape he would surely have underled at trick two, to get his ruff. In all other cases where the finesse works, the squeeze also works; and there is no guess. At the point of decision you will know that West started with three hearts and seven diamonds. Since one round of clubs and two rounds of spades will have been played, his entire distribution will be known.

Results

If you overruffed and played trumps from your hand, plus 620. (You'd get the ending right.) If not, minus 100. (East is good enough to find the correct defense.)

Board 5

North dealer
North–South vulnerable

You, South, hold:

♠ 54   ♡ 8742   ◊ 109742   ♣ Q5

SOUTH	WEST	NORTH	EAST
—	—	1♣	1♠
Pass	2♣[1]	Pass	2NT
Pass	3♠	Pass	4♠
Pass	Pass	Pass	

[1] General force

What do you lead?

```
                    NORTH
                    ♠ A
                    ♡ AK53
                    ◇ Q86
                    ♣ J9862
     WEST                          EAST
     ♠ J9863                       ♠ KQ1072
     ♡ Q10                         ♡ J96
     ◇ AJ3                         ◇ K5
     ♣ K103                        ♣ A74
                    SOUTH
                    ♠ 54
                    ♡ 8742
                    ◇ 109742
                    ♣ Q5
```

This deal will be cherished by cultists devoted to underleading doubleton queens. Every decade or so, these leads works, sending the enthusiasts into ecstasy. If you wish to consider such leads, here are the positions in which they are most likely to succeed: (a) from a weak hand, when real strength has been shown on your left; (b) into declarer's known honor strength in the suit (in this deal, for example, where East has bid notrump over a club bid, the low lead might find East with king–jack third; the scenario is for North to win the opening lead with the club ace and return the suit, hoping that South led a singleton: declarer finesses the jack, not knowing what to expect but definitely not expecting what follows, which is that North regains the lead with a side ace and gives South a club ruff!); (c) whenever it works (see diagram). What these cases have in common is that the opening leader has a very weak hand.

Results

If you led the club five, plus 50 (but beware of the Dark of the Moon). If not, minus 420 (and a mind at ease).

Board 6

East dealer
East–West vulnerable

> **NORTH**
> ♠ KQJ9
> ♡ K73
> ◊ KQ
> ♣ QJ62
>
> **SOUTH**
> ♠ 753
> ♡ A9
> ◊ A643
> ♣ AK104

You open one notrump and partner bids two clubs, Stayman. After your two–diamond response partner leaps to six notrump. The play proceeds:

> *Heart queen, three, deuce, **ace**.*
> *Spade seven, deuce, **king**, four.*
> *Club six, seven, **king**, three.*
> *Spade five, six, queen, **ace**.*
> *Heart four, nine, ten, **king**.*
> *Diamond **king**, five, three, deuce.*
> *Diamond **queen**, seven, four, eight.*
> *Club **queen**, nine, four, five.*
> *Club **jack**, heart five, ten, eight.*
> *Club deuce, heart six, **club ace**, heart jack.*
> *Diamond **ace**, jack, heart seven, nine.*
> *Spade three, eight, ?*

There! We've done all the hard work, playing eleven and a half tricks for you. All you have to do is play one card.

Which one?

```
                    NORTH
                    ♠ KQJ9
                    ♡ K73
                    ◇ KQ
                    ♣ QJ62
    WEST                            EAST
    ♠ 862                           ♠ A104
    ♡ QJ108                         ♡ 6542
    ◇ J82                           ◇ 10975
    ♣ 853                           ♣ 97
                    SOUTH
                    ♠ 753
                    ♡ A9
                    ◇ A643
                    ♣ AK104
```

In this sort of set–up, the quality of the opposition has a substantial bearing on the play most likely to succeed. For example, an inexperienced West would be unlikely to discard the jack of hearts at any time, and especially before throwing a useless diamond, unless under pressure (so maybe he is long in spades). However, a good player would realize that it will be fatal to the defense for declarer to be able to place any non–spade card in the West hand at trick twelve. So, West must get that jack of hearts out of his hand; he cannot set the contract if he keeps it. (Similarly, it would have been puerile for West to cover the nine of hearts with the jack, keeping the ten of hearts as one of his last two cards — declarer is not likely to believe in an opening lead from queen jack–eight, when relatively safe leads were available elsewhere.)

In fact, looking over all the plays made by East–West, with the knowledge that they are good players, you realize that they have told you nothing they didn't have to. They are not going to signal their distribution for your benefit; East would have had to take his spade ace both from ace–four and ace–ten–four. The opening lead and heart return were automatic. The discarding was effective.

Well, if the opponents refuse to tell us what we want to know, how can we determine the best play? There is little choice but to fall back on the percentages. Happily, once we recognize which cards the opponents were forced to play, the calculation is easy. In the suit of "spades below the ten," all of which we drew. West had three and East one. However, East had the ace of spades. In the suit of heart honors, all of which had to be played, West had all three.

Similarly, in the suit of "hearts below the seven," all of which were forced to show up, East had all four. Finally, West had three clubs and East two. (The information from the diamond plays, which can be considered random subject only to the mild condition that the six not become established, tells you that some unknown defender started with four and the other with three.)

Adding it all up, West started with nine known cards to East's eight. So, East is more likely to have been dealt the ten of spades.

What would you do if the calculation indicated that the chances were equal?

You should play for the drop — you go down one less when you are wrong.

Results

If you played for the drop, plus 990. If you finessed, minus 100.

Board 7

South dealer
Both vulnerable

You, South, hold:

♠ A86   ♡ 5   ◇ AK10942   ♣ 1065

SOUTH	WEST	NORTH	EAST
1◇	Pass	1♡	Pass
2◇	Pass	2NT	Pass
?			

What call do you make?

```
                    NORTH
                    ♠ Q75
                    ♡ AQ864
                    ◇ 3
                    ♣ K974
     WEST                          EAST
     ♠ J1032                       ♠ K94
     ♡ KJ9                         ♡ 10732
     ◇ J876                        ◇ Q5
     ♣ Q2                          ♣ AJ83
                    SOUTH
                    ♠ A86
                    ♡ 5
                    ◇ AK10942
                    ♣ 1065
```

Don't pass. There is a good chance that if you can't make three notrump then you can't make two notrump either. Or, to put it another way, you are more likely to make three diamonds than two notrump. The choice should be between three notrump and three diamonds.

The risk of three notrump is that the contract may well go down more than one, and it goes down in hundreds. So, the usual highly favorable odds in favor of bidding vulnerable games at IMPs, which assume that a loss will be down one, do not apply. If three diamonds makes while three notrump will either make or go down, say, 300, the imp odds in favor of bidding game are only 10 to 9.

However, we believe three notrump is the decision that will be reached through correct hand evaluation, in particularly the valuation of the ten–nine of diamonds. If partner has a diamond fit, or partial diamond fit, the powerful suit and quick side trick will give a good chance for nine tricks. If partner has a misfit for diamonds, he must have solid high–card values for the invitation.

There must be a good chance he can hold the fort while the diamonds spots, in conjunction with the probably unassailable spade–ace entry, bring in the suit: six tricks from you, three from him.

Of course. it also doesn't hurt to catch a lucky lie of the cards. However, against a good team you can expect the opposition to make the aggressive move and get the same breaks.

Results

If you passed, plus 150. If you bid three diamonds, plus 110. If you bid three notrump (or three spades), plus 600.

Post–Mortem

Board 1

While your table had a minor–suit part–score battle, one of your teammates tried an experiment.

NORTH
♠ J4
♡ AK862
◇ AQ743
♣ 2

WEST
♠ 973
♡ QJ1097
◇ 5
♣ J873

EAST
♠ AQ108
♡ 4
◇ KJ9
♣ AK964

SOUTH
♠ K652
♡ 53
◇ 10862
♣ Q105

SOUTH	WEST	NORTH	EAST
—	—	1♡	Double
Pass	Pass	Pass	

East led a trump. Declarer won, and played on diamonds; he had to lose two diamonds, two black aces, and three trump tricks. North–South minus 100.

Board 2

Where you had to duck your ace of spades in tempo in order to give declarer adequate opportunity to go down at four hearts, your teammates did not stretch towards their potential game.

SOUTH	WEST	NORTH	EAST
—	—	—	Pass
Pass	1♠	Pass	1NT
Pass	2♡	Pass	Pass
Pass			

The play started similarly. North won the second trick with the spade queen. North–South minus 140.

Board 3

Where you had to play third–hand–low to defeat a normal three–notrump contract, the player in your seat did not have to face the challenge.

NORTH
- ♠ J762
- ♡ K107
- ◇ 9854
- ♣ 43

WEST
- ♠ A85
- ♡ AJ62
- ◇ AKQ
- ♣ Q97

EAST
- ♠ Q94
- ♡ 53
- ◇ 1032
- ♣ KJ1086

SOUTH
- ♠ K103
- ♡ Q984
- ◇ J76
- ♣ A52

After two notrump—three notrump—all pass, North led the eight of diamonds. Declarer (West) won, and attacked clubs. South took the third round of clubs: after some thought, he returned a diamond. Declarer won and tried a spade to the queen. (The play might have been more interesting if South had shifted to hearts.)

North–South plus 200.

Board 4

Where you had to maneuver a trump squeeze to make four hearts, your partner's bidding problem was solved differently.

West dealer
Both vulnerable

NORTH
♠ A643
♡ 7
◇ Q74
♣ AK652

WEST
♠ Q97
♡ 54
◇ AK108632
♣ J

EAST
♠ J1052
♡ K986
◇ J
♣ Q1093

SOUTH
♠ K8
♡ AQJ1032
◇ 95
♣ 764

SOUTH	WEST	NORTH	EAST
—	3◇	Pass	Pass
3♡	Pass	3NT	Pass
Pass	Pass		

Do you approve of North's three–notrump bid?

It's anybody's guess. The hand doesn't look notrumpy to us. We sort of like four clubs, which opens up new possibilities. However, we doubt anyone could make out a really good case for any particular call as right. If someone suggested passing, for example, could we say that was definitely wrong?

Do you approve of South's leave-in of three notrump?

We do. There is enough firepower if hearts run. If not, the king of spades may be a speedy enough entry. Furthermore, the doubleton diamond is a negative sign for hearts, suggesting the possibility of a defensive ruff.

East led his diamond. West won and shifted to a spade, but it did no good. Declarer bounced up ace of spades, cleared hearts, and took two spades, five hearts and two clubs.

North–South plus 600.

Board 5

Where you could have defeated four spades by under-leading the doubleton queen, your straight–down–the–sides teammates had no trouble avoiding the five–five major–suit fit.

```
                    NORTH
                    ♠ A
                    ♡ AK53
                    ◇ Q86
                    ♣ J9862
    WEST                              EAST
    ♠ J9863                           ♠ KQ1072
    ♡ Q10                             ♡ J96
    ◇ AJ3                             ◇ K5
    ♣ K103                            ♣ A74
                    SOUTH
                    ♠ 54
                    ♡ 8742
                    ◇ 109742
                    ♣ Q5
```

SOUTH	WEST	NORTH	EAST
—	—	1♣	1♠
Pass	2♣ [1]	Pass	2♠
Pass	2NT	Pass	3NT
Pass	Pass	Pass	

[1] Strong spade raise

Once West had announced his spade support unequivocally, early in the auction, he was able to describe the general nature of his hand. An interesting sequence.

A heart lead would have held declarer to his contract, but North led a club, reasonably enough. Later, North was squeezed and endplayed out of everything but his underwear.

North–South minus 430. (Top on the board!)

Board 6

Where you faced a drop–finesse–squeeze sort of guess at six notrump, the player with your cards opened with a 15–17 point notrump. Responder tried Stayman, then an invitational four notrump, passed out. The play went similarly, and declarer guessed right at the end. You wisely congratulate your teammates on their discarding, especially since they put forth a good effort when only an overtrick was at stake. North–South plus 490.

Board 7

Where you were presented with the decision of whether or not to bid game on,

♠ A86   ♡ 5   ◇ AK10942   ♣ 1065,

your counterparts had the same auction.

SOUTH	WEST	NORTH	EAST
1◇	Pass	1♡	Pass
2◇	Pass	2NT	Pass
?			

and their final decision was to raise two notrump to three notrump. North–South plus 600.

□   □   □

Have you become a temporary folk hero by slaying the visiting dragons? If not, did you at least give a good account of yourself, so you can hope to play on a dragon team someday?

Match Six

Off to the Nationals

"YOU CAN'T STAY HOME FOREVER." Or is it, "You can't go home again"? No matter. Either way, it's off to the Nationals! Spearheaded by your partner's optimism and enthusiasm, you have been knocking them dead in local events. This encourages you to venture afield, and spend a substantial chunk of your hard—earned money to take a look at the big time. Not the really big time—no national knockout just yet, thank you. But you will play in some pair games and, of course, the National Swiss. Your other pair? Not to worry, you'll meet someone there.

Your partner's system is three parts Bridge World Standard and one part random, flamboyant over bidding. Admittedly, some good card handling goes along with this, and the overaggressiveness has proved very effective against run—of—the—mill competition. You can't help wondering if wildness might not get its come- uppance against more talented opposition.

The pair you pick up seems quite suitable. They are sociable, but very intense about the game. They use a relatively simple system, but they seem to analyze the deals very carefully, usually marking their scorecards with cryptic indications in at least three different colors, and filing them amidst a mass of pens, pencils and papers.

The National Swiss is a four—session event: two qualifying, two final. You have to be in the top 40% of the field after the first two sessions (eight matches) in order to play in the final, where there will be full carry—over. Scoring is by win—loss; you get three—quarters if you win by 1 or 2 imps; only an exact IMP tie gives you a half a point. (For this foolish scoring you had to come all the way to a National?)

Since almost everyone in the event is a stranger to you, it is hard to judge the caliber of your opposition. Your first–round opponents seem competent; they play you level, but their teammates make several elementary blunders against yours, and you win easily. In the second round, your opponents are less impressive. The boards are very dull, there are no big swings, and your team is lucky to win, 7–3, on tiny differences and overtricks. Not much chance, in either match, to judge the skills of your teammates. But 2–0 is a good start.

Now it's round three. More strangers to play against. All you know is that they, also, have won two matches in the vast sea of bridge players that the event comprises.

Board 8

West dealer
None vulnerable

<pre>
                    NORTH
                    ♠ —
                    ♡ 632
                    ◇ AKQ52
                    ♣ AK972

                    SOUTH
                    ♠ J95
                    ♡ A874
                    ◇ 96
                    ♣ Q1054
</pre>

SOUTH	WEST	NORTH	EAST
—	Pass	1◇	Pass
1♡	Pass	3♣	Pass
3◇	Pass	4♣	Pass
4♡	Pass	Pass	Pass

Not exactly a meeting of the minds on the meaning of the sequence! Are all those expenses to go for nothing?

West leads the spade six

Plan the play.

NORTH
♠ —
♡ 632
◇ AKQ52
♣ AK972

WEST
♠ K87643
♡ Q10
◇ J103
♣ J8

EAST
♠ AQ102
♡ KJ95
◇ 874
♣ 63

SOUTH
♠ J95
♡ A874
◇ 96
♣ Q1054

This will be a difficult test for you. Not because four–three trump contracts are so difficult. but because it is hard to concentrate after a partnership misunderstanding. Nonetheless, effective players overcome these problems. The important thing is not to let yourself be upset to such an extent that it prevents you from playing your best either here or on any subsequent board.

In the silly four–heart contract at hand, if you panic and go about making tricks as fast as possible, you will suffer for your lack of foresight: spade ruff, club queen, spade ruff, three diamonds (they live), another high club perhaps. Then there you are in dummy, and in trouble. There is no escape, whatever the distribution of the missing cards; nor would it help to ruff the third diamond and take another spade ruff. A possible im- provement on this general plan is to finesse the club ten at trick two. If clubs are two–two with the jack onside, this would provide a later reentry needed to play two rounds of trumps (you would still need a three–three trump break, else you would lose control).

A simpler plan, based on keeping control of the trump suit, will succeed when diamonds are three–three, and trumps not worse than four–two. Ruff the opening lead in dummy, and duck a round of trumps. If things are breaking right for you, the defenders will be helpless. If they play a second trump, you win the ace, and play (you hope) four rounds of diamonds, getting rid of your two losing spades before the defense regains the lead. (If the defense slips by playing a spade at trick three, you ruff in dummy, come to the club queen, cash the heart ace, and play three top diamonds, succeeding even if diamonds are four–two.)

A superior line is to run three rounds of diamonds before touching trumps, pitching a spade from the closed hand; if the diamonds are three–three, declarer reverts to ducking a trump. This line will cost if clubs are four–zero, or if one opponent has two hearts and one club, since a club return would scramble communications and allow the hand with the short trump to get a ruff; but both distributions are very unlikely, considering the silence of the nonvulnerable opponents

If the diamonds are four–two you have several chances. When the defender with the doubleton makes the mistake of ruffing the third round of diamonds, you are cold, unless the ruff is with a doubleton trump. Win the trump return (as good as any), ruff the last spade in dummy, cross back to a club, and play a trump, losing only three trump tricks. When the hand with the doubleton diamond refuses to ruff (a far from obvious defense), duck a round of trumps, win the trump return, and play a third round of trumps, hoping for a three–three split.

Results

If you played to ruff spades in dummy, minus 50. If you finessed the ten or clubs, minus 100. If you ducked a round of trumps, before or after three diamonds, plus 420.

Board 9

Partner is the dealer
Opponents vulnerable

You, South, hold:

♠ AKQ3   ♡ 742   ◇ J1095   ♣ 86

Partner, the dealer, passes. RHO opens one club.

What call do you make?

Few textbooks will advise it, but you have to be pretty chicken not to bid one spade. If partner bids too high, presumably on a spade fit, your concentration of honor strength will prevent his sacrifice from being a phantom—a slight oversave. 800 against game, say, is only a medium loss. And there is plenty to gain. You may disrupt the opponents' auction, whether partner can raise or not. If partner is strong, your side may be able to compete. Partner may be attracted to a spade lead. And the opponents may fail to try for three notrump for fear of your presumed long suit.

Over your one-spade overcall, the bidding continues:

YOU	LHO	PARTNER	RHO
—	—	Pass	1♣
1♠	2♦	Pass	2♡
Pass	3♦	Pass	3♡
Pass	4♡	Pass	Pass
Pass			

DUMMY (LHO)
♠ J98
♡ 653
♦ AKQ742
♣ 10

YOU
♠ AKQ3
♡ 742
♦ J1095
♣ 86

You lead and win the king, queen, ace of spades. Partner
plays two, seven, five. Declarer plays four, six, ten. So far,
so good.

Now what?

NORTH
- ♠ 752
- ♡ 1098
- ◊ 83
- ♣ QJ974

WEST
- ♠ J98
- ♡ 653
- ◊ AKQ742
- ♣ 10

EAST
- ♠ 1064
- ♡ AKQJ
- ◊ 6
- ♣ AK532

SOUTH
- ♠ AKQ3
- ♡ 742
- ◊ J1095
- ♣ 86

Your trumps are too weak for the thirteenth spade to do any good. One choice is to lead a diamond, which will cut declarer's link to dummy if the closed hand has 3–4–1–5 distribution; this holds East to two diamond tricks, defeating the contract if East's clubs (or trumps) aren't strong enough (see diagram). Or, you might lead a club, to avoid doing any damage with a diamond lead.

What damage could a diamond lead do? Well, suppose declarer's hand were something like,

♠ 1064   ♡ AQJxx   ◊ —   ♣ AKxxx

If you lead a diamond, East will maneuver trump finesses, take discards, ruff once in dummy, and never come to the edge of the Valley of Death. However, if you exit with a club, declarer will win the club, ruff a club in dummy, take a necessary discard, finesse in trumps, and then . . . ? Now, declarer has to guess whether to try to get back to dummy what another club ruff for another trump finesse, or to try to drop the heart king doubleton.

Despite this possibility, the indicated defense is the diamond switch. This may be essential when declarer has the appropriate hand type, and unconditionally so. Declarer, with the 3–5–0–5 hand, might not have opened one club (most wouldn't), might have passed three diamonds (though most wouldn't), and might not guess wrong even if presented with the appropriate problem.

Results

If you did anything other than overcall one spade over one club, minus 600. It you overcalled one spade, plus 100 if you shifted to a diamond at trick four; minus 620 otherwise.

Board 10

RHO is the dealer
Both vulnerable

You, South, hold:

♠ KQ2   ♡ 64   ◇ AKJ106   ♣ 975

RHO the dealer, opens two hearts, weak.

What call do you make?

We have no strong feelings about this one. We like to use light takeout doubles over weak two–bids, just as over one–bids. However, with balanced hands we are more cautious. There has to be some point at which you have enough safety to double one heart but not enough safety (because of level) to double two hearts with a balanced hand. Here, we would not criticize either a pass or a double. (Three diamonds is too restrictive, as well as unnecessarily dangerous.) A double could get you into big trouble it your side is outgunned, or could get you into ordinary trouble in clubs. As against that, this may be your side's last safe chance to enter the auction.

We'll suppose you pass. LHO raises to four hearts, and all pass.

DUMMY (LHO)
♠ J106
♡ Q975
♢ 8
♣ AK432

YOU
♠ KQ2
♡ 64
♢ AKJ106
♣ 975

You lead the king of diamonds: eight, deuce, five.

Plan your defense.

```
                    NORTH
                    ♠ A532
                    ♡ 8
                    ◇ 9732
                    ♣ QJ108
     WEST                          EAST
     ♠ J106                        ♠ 987
     ♡ Q975                        ♡ AKJ1032
     ◇ 8                           ◇ Q54
     ♣ AK432                       ♣ 6
                    SOUTH
                    ♠ KQ4
                    ♡ 64
                    ◇ AKJ106
                    ♣ 975
```

Whatever East has in clubs, the suit will provide tricks sooner or later. So, partner needs the ace of spades (suggested by the discouraging diamond) for the contract to be defeatable. You plan to lead the spade king (the deuce–lead is all right also) and then the deuce. Partner will win and, perforce, return a third spade. If declarer has another spade, you will defeat the contract.

You must not play the king of spades followed by the queen. Partner would be entitled to play you for a doubleton, overtaking the second spade to give you a ruff (necessary if East started with 4–6–3–0 distribution—it's not for North to reason why East opened two hearts, only to follow your indicated defense). Partner should assume you would make a "partnership safety play" of low the second time without a doubleton.

Results

If you overcalled three diamonds, minus 500 (at five diamonds doubled). Otherwise, if you played deuce, or king–deuce of spades, plus 100: if not, minus 620.

Board 11

South dealer
None vulnerable

You, South, hold:

♠ None   ♡ A10862   ◇ A42   ♣ AQJ85

You open one heart: LHO passes; partner leaps to four hearts: RHO comes in with four spades.

What call do you make?

Clearly you must compete further, since your offense is much greater than your defense. Probably, five hearts is no worse than a finesse (and a club finesse is likely to win). Meanwhile, defensive prospects against spades are uncertain, perhaps depending more on the opponents' distribution than anything else.

Since slam is possible, and your side may be called upon to make a later decision over further spade bids, your indicated action is five clubs. You certainly don't want partner to sell out with a club–heart two–suiter; this is the best way to send that message.

You bid five clubs, LHO joins in with five spades, which is passed back to you.

What call do you make?

Your new–suit bid suggested that it is "your hand." If partner doesn't want to double five spades you, with your spade void, all first–round controls, outside source of tricks, and with your only weakness—trumps—likely covered by partner (considering the triple raise), don't want to double either. The simplest action is six hearts. Partner might misinterpret your intentions if you did anything else.

You bid six hearts. LHO surprises you by continuing to six spades. Partner doubles. RHO passes.

What do you do now?

You've had enough. Partner would not have been so timid with the cards to make seven a sensible contract.

Against six spades doubled, what do you lead?

NORTH
♠ 97
♡ KQ754
◇ Q762
♣ 106

WEST
♠ 8543
♡ J9
◇ KJ1095
♣ 32

EAST
♠ AKQJ1062
♡ 3
◇ 8
♣ K974

SOUTH
♠ —
♡ A10862
◇ A43
♣ AQJ85

We see no reason to lead anything but a heart. However, we see plenty of reasons to lead a low one. Partner may be able to gain the lead to play a club through declarer's (hypothetical) king before trumps are drawn, and before the ace of diamonds is dislodged. One way or another, this may add to our total of club tricks (possibly including ruffs). Is there any substantial risk involved in this underlead? Almost none, in our opinion. It's a moral certainty that West doesn't have the heart king for his bidding. It's highly unlikely East has it for his. More important, partner is almost guaranteed to hold the king for the forcing pass over five spades. The four-heart bid was supposed to show good trumps; within that context, one would hardly think of any queen–high trump holding as slam–positive. It must be 99% that partner has the king. So, the possible gain by under-leading clearly outweighs any possible loss.

Results

If you led the heart ace (or a low diamond, or any club), plus 300. If you led the diamond ace, plus 800. If you underled the heart ace, plus 1100 (but take a black mark if you didn't choose a very low one, since this should be a suit–preference signal: we choose not to discuss whether the six or the two is the better lead).

If you doubled five spades, subtract one undertrick. If you bid over six spades, add one undertrick—you pegged West correctly! By the way, you can make seven hearts. Do you think you would have?

Board 12

LHO is the dealer
Your side vulnerable

DUMMY (RHO)
♠ KQ10
♡ —
♢ AQJ10
♣ AJ8642

YOU
♠ A53
♡ J1082
♢ 764
♣ KQ9

LHO	PARTNER	RHO	YOU
1♡	Pass	2♣	Pass
2♡	Pass	3♢	Pass
3♡	Pass	3NT	Pass
4♡	Pass	Pass	Pass

Partner leads the spade four; king from dummy.

Plan your defense.

```
                    NORTH
                    ♠ 97642
                    ♡ K3
                    ◇ 985
                    ♣ 753
WEST                                    EAST
♠ J8                                    ♠ KQ10
♡ AQ97654                               ♡ —
◇ K32                                   ◇ AQJ10
♣ 10                                    ♣ AJ8642
                    SOUTH
                    ♠ A53
                    ♡ J1082
                    ◇ 764
                    ♣ KQ9
```

If West's hearts are headed by ace–king–queen, the party's over. (Declarer can take a finesse if necessary.) If partner has one of the honors, declarer must have the king of diamonds, and so has no side–suit problems.

Therefore, the first part of your plan should be to take the ace of spades at trick one. There is no particular reason not to, and ducking might lose if the declarer's distribution were, for example, 2–7–2–2. (Among other possibilities, declarer might shake the jack of spades on a diamond, then take a ruffing finesse in spades for a club pitch.)

The next part of your plan revolves around getting three defensive trump tricks. No sweat if partner's (presumed) honor is the ace; no hope if it's the queen. What if it's the king? With that shoddy a heart suit, declarer will surely have seven. West can drop partner's doubleton king, and you can be sure this will happen if you play the deuce of hearts under the ace (West will have no reason to do otherwise).

However, if you hide your deuce declarer will have something to think about. Your most effective play is likely to be the eight. If honest, that is twice as likely to be from jack–eight or ten–eight as from king–eight; this suggests that declarer play the queen on the second round. (If you drop, say, the ten, declarer has to compare only honest plays from jack–ten and king–ten.) Still, this is a very tricky situation. In practice, your best falsecard depends in part on your estimation of declarer's estimation of your level of skill.

Results

If you defended correctly on Board 10 and you underled on Board 11, minus 420 regardless (declarer has learned to respect you). Otherwise, minus 420 unless you planned to play the eight or hearts on the first round of trumps, in which case plus 50.

Board 13

North dealer
Both vulnerable

You, South, hold:

♠ K9543   ♡ AJ   ◇ Q87   ♣ 1062

SOUTH	WEST	NORTH	EAST
—	—	1 ♡	Pass
1 ♠	Pass	2 ◇	Pass
?			

What call do you make?

```
                    NORTH
                    ♠ 7
                    ♡ Q9654
                    ◊ AK65
                    ♣ K74
    WEST                            EAST
    ♠ Q106                          ♠ AJ82
    ♡ K102                          ♡ 873
    ◊ J942                          ◊ 103
    ♣ Q95                           ♣ AJ83
                    SOUTH
                    ♠ K9543
                    ♡ AJ
                    ◊ Q87
                    ♣ 1062
```

When a wide variety of options are available, it is usually best to avoid the extremes. One extreme action is pass (great danger of missing game when partner has extra values, since the South hand not only has high–card strength but also fitting honors in North's suits). Another is a high forcing action such as three clubs, an unnecessary overbid since you probably can reach game anyway when it is cold.

The moderate actions are two hearts, two spades, two notrump and three diamonds. Naturally, there is something seriously wrong with all of them. Three diamonds is a raise with inadequate support, and it increases the bidding level. Two notrump is all right on values (considering the fitting honors), but there is weakness in the unbid suit. Two spades is grossly misdirected with such weak spades and good red suits. Two hearts is the indicated strain, but fails to show additional values.

Since you want to have a good chance to make what-ever you bid opposite a minimum, three diamonds and two spades are unattractive. The choice is between the aggressive two notrump and the conservative two hearts.

We have no strong choice between them, and it is clear that neither is perfect. On a bad day, if you bid two notrump partner will have an absolute minimum, and will go down 200 after the best lead, while he would have made two hearts on a trump coup. However, if you bid two hearts, partner, with perhaps bad hearts and good everything else, will pass when three notrump is solid. Partner and vulnerability may also affect the decision. With your present partner, two hearts may be enough. Others would stretch to two notrump because vulnerable though if partner stretches also you may find yourself in a game bid more on the vulnerability than on card values.

Results

Action	Contract	Lead	Score
Pass	2♦	♦10	+90
2♡	2♡	♦10	+110
2♠	2♠	♣5	-100
2NT	2NT	♦2[1]	+120
3♣	3NT(N)	♣3	-100
3♦	3♦	♦10	-100
3♡	4♡	♦10	-200

[1] Yes, we see how to beat it looking at all four hands.

Board 14

East dealer
None vulnerable

You, South, hold:

♠ 64   ♡ 8   ◇ AKJ862   ♣ KQ104

SOUTH	WEST	NORTH	EAST
—	—	—	1♡
2◇	Double	3◇	4♡
?			

What call do you make?

```
                    NORTH
                    ♠ K875
                    ♡ 1062
                    ◊ Q1053
                    ♣ J6
    WEST                            EAST
    ♠ A1092                         ♠ QJ3
    ♡ J4                            ♡ AKQ9753
    ◊ 74                            ◊ 9
    ♣ A8532                         ♣ 97
                    SOUTH
                    ♠ 64
                    ♡ 8
                    ◊ AKJ862
                    ♣ KQ104
```

In judging an intended sacrifice where you cannot gauge the opponents' prospects too accurately, you can still make an attempt to measure gain or loss by calculating your own prospects. The normal number of tricks to take in diamonds would be ten. A normal hand for partner would be something to fill the diamonds plus an ace, or equivalent value. Usually, that will come to ten tricks (though, of course, it will not always do so). Assuming that, what are the IMP odds on a sacrifice? If the opponents can make 420, a sacrifice of 100 shows a profit of 320, 8 imps; if the opponents are going down, say 50, a sacrifice of 100 shows a loss of 150, 4 imps. Even though this entire calculation is over simplified, it is sensible to use the result as an approximation of reality. The IMP odds in favor of a one–trick sacrifice are 8 to 4 (or 2 to 1). Is it 2 to 1 that the opponents will go down? Probably not, so a five–diamond bid is indicated.

Results

If you pass, minus 420. If you bid five diamonds, minus 100 (West doubles and East passes).

Post–Mortem

Board 8

Where your pair perpetrated an obscure sequence to reach a flaky Moysian fit, your opposite numbers found the right suit, but . . .

NORTH
♠ —
♡ 632
◇ AKQ52
♣ AK972

SOUTH
♠ J95
♡ A874
◇ 96
♣ Q1054

SOUTH	NORTH
—	1◇
1♡	2♣
Pass	

North–South plus an embarrassing 190.

Whose error?

Some would say no one goofed. North–South were unlucky to have a perfect fit. South would have bid the same way with, for example, three queens, in which case any game might be headed for defeat.

Yes, sometimes you just don't have enough room to discover your potential without risking too much. However, there is such a thing as a "percentage action" which will work out best over the long run. We think North's percentage action is to jump shift. The heart fit makes the loss of game too likely after a mere two–club rebid.

Board 9

Where you defended against a 4–3 four–heart contract, your teammates avoided game with their 27 HCP.

NORTH
♠ 752
♡ 1098
◇ 83
♣ QJ874

WEST
♠ J98
♡ 653
◇ AKQ742
♣ 10

EAST
♠ 1064
♡ AKQJ
◇ 6
♣ AK532

SOUTH
♠ AKQ3
♡ 742
◇ J1095
♣ 86

SOUTH	WEST	NORTH	EAST
—	—	Pass	1♣
1♠	2♢	Pass	2♡
Pass	3♢	Pass	Pass
Pass			

East's dramatically conservative move was based on the deduction that partner had weak spade length, but it did little good. North led a spade. South took three rounds and, with nothing to lose looking at the dummy, played a fourth round. North's eight of diamonds provided the setting trick.

North–South plus 100.

Board 10

Where you had to engineer a defensive cashout against four hearts, your teammates (whose two–heart opening is Flannery) found a way to stop under game.

SOUTH	WEST	NORTH	EAST
–	–	–	Pass
1♢	Pass	1♠	2♡
Pass	3♢	Pass	3♡
Pass	Pass	Pass	

Three diamonds, a cue–bid used as a strong raise, showed "more strength in diamonds than in spades." Again deducing, from South's surprising failure to raise, that partner had long weak spades. East pulled in a notch. "We specialize in three small spades in each hand." East remarks.

North–South minus 140.

Board 11

Where you had a chance to pick up a lot of points with an underlead against a sacrifice contract, your partner's aggressive preempt with no singleton was not duplicated in the other room.

SOUTH	WEST	NORTH	EAST
1♡	Pass	3♡	4♠
5♣	Pass	5♡	Pass
Pass	Pass		

North–South plus 480.

Board 12

Where you had the opportunity to falsecard with the eight of trumps from J–I0–8–2 against four hearts, the player in your chair failed to find this move in an identical position. This gave declarer no alternative to the winning play in trumps.

North–South minus 420.

Board 13

Where you had an awkward rebid problem with a 10–point hand:

♠ K9543   ♡ AJ   ◇ Q87   ♣ 1062

The auction in the other room was:

SOUTH	WEST	NORTH	EAST
—	—	1♡	Pass
1♠	Pass	1NT	Pass
Pass	Pass		

East led a low club.

North–South plus 120.

Board 14

Where you had to decide whether or not to sacrifice at five diamonds, the players in your seats did sacrifice, but the circumstances were different.

NORTH
♠ K875
♡ 1062
♢ Q1053
♣ J6

WEST
♠ A1092
♡ J4
♢ 74
♣ A8532

EAST
♠ QJ3
♡ AKQ9753
♢ 9
♣ 97

SOUTH
♠ 64
♡ 8
♢ AKJ862
♣ KQ104

SOUTH	WEST	NORTH	EAST
—	—	—	1 ♡
3 ♢[1]	Double[2]	5 ♢	5 ♡
Pass	Pass	Pass	

[1] Intermediate
[2] Negative

South led the king of diamonds and switched smartly to the king of clubs.

North–South plus 50.

Who else goofed for East–West?

It is easy to see that East–West would have been better off, as a matter of overall strategy, bidding six hearts instead of five. This depends (essentially) on the same finesse as five hearts, counts 500 more when you make it, and loses only 50 more when you don't. And that finesse, on the auction, is better than 50%. However, it

164

is hard to analyze such things even in a noncompetitive sequence. Each individual action taken by East and West seems quite reasonable.

What about the difference between five hearts and five diamonds doubled? As with the analysis for the sacrificing side, we can try to get some idea of the IMP odds. With the spade finesse losing, bidding five hearts cost East–West 4 imps (50 plus the 100 they could have had doubling five diamonds). If the spade finesse had been onside, it is a reasonable approximation that five diamonds doubled would have gone down 300, while five hearts would have scored 480 for a gain of 5 imps. Since, if anything, the spade finesse was better than an even chance, East–West had at worst a reasonable expectation at five hearts, once the opponents had sacrificed.

□   □   □

By this time, you should have all the scores figured. Is your team still undefeated?

Match Seven

Second–Half Slump

YOU ARE FULL OF ANTICIPATION when you make your first appearance at a Sectional, for the second session of a one–day Swiss teams. Unfortunately, your teammates— the usual bunch, not much better nor much worse than most other players in the event—have disheartening news. They have scored a mediocre 2–2 in the afternoon session, and nobody wants to talk about it much.

However, your worst player has now gone home; though not mentioning that directly, you point out, cheerily, how the team can still get in the money with a bunch of wins in the evening. Unfortunately, things go rapidly from bad to worse. In the first evening match, against a weak team, your opponents make two gross errors; one breaks even, the other gains three imps for them. Meanwhile, your teammates misdefend a game down off the top. An easy loss. In Match Six, you bid a slam needing a finesse plus no five–zero break. The finesse loses. Your teammates bid a vulnerable game that needs finesse and a three–two split. Their finesse loses too. Your team is now 2–4; it is definitely not your day.

It will be hard to put forth your best effort in the next match, because you are playing almost entirely for personal pride. There will be a tendency to relax. Still, you don't want to let the bridge deteriorate; every session of hard thinking you log makes you that much stronger in future events. Anyway, your motivation is enhanced by the opponents for this seventh match. They are a group similar to yours in skill; one of them is an occasional member of better teams in the area—you would like to do well against him. Places are chosen, and the capable player is seated at your right. Your partner, who looks bored, plays Bridge World Standard with a few personal frills.

Board 1

Partner deals: neither side is vulnerable. Partner passes. RHO opens one diamond, and you overcall one heart holding.

♠ A4 ♡ AJ7642 ◇ A8 ♣ K65.

After two passes, RHO reopens with one notrump.

What call do you make?

Pass, double and two hearts are all within reason. Two hearts, with such a weak suit, is an overbid (and slightly dangerous, since LHO can double now that RHO has shown strength, and some hearts). Furthermore, if you can make two hearts you can probably beat one notrump—it is unnecessary to bid. Doubling is overaggressive since you really have no reason to believe your hand better than RHO's.

We'll assume that you pass one notrump. So, too, does everyone else.

DUMMY (LHO)
♠ KJ6
♡ 53
◇ 6432
♣ 8743

YOU
♠ A4
♡ AJ7642
◇ A8
♣ K65

You led the heart six, and dummy appears.

Should dummy have taken out to two diamonds?

We don't know. That's one of life's imponderables. Two diamonds may get to a better contract, but it might also stir up the animals—opponents have a way of perking up their ears when a minor–suit fit is revealed at a low level. Anyway, one notrump looks to be a favorite, since this is going to be good dummy—more than its share of high cards (on the auction), plus some diamond length that may help establish winners. How bad can it be?

On trick one, partner plays the ten and declarer wins with the king. He leads the queen of diamonds from his hand.

What do you play?

You can't afford to duck. If declarer has his bid, partner can't have the king of diamonds, so you have no hope of getting him on lead quickly in diamonds. However, partner could have something like jack–third in diamonds; declarer might not get it right on the next round, but . . .

You win the ace of diamonds, and partner plays the five.

Now what?

NORTH
♠ 109753
♡ 108
◇ 975
♣ Q109

WEST
♠ KJ6
♡ 53
◇ 6432
♣ 8743

EAST
♠ Q82
♡ KQ9
◇ KQJ10
♣ AJ2

SOUTH
♠ A4
♡ AJ7642
◇ A8
♣ K65

Declarer is marked with queen–nine of hearts, so partner must have a black queen to defeat the contract (if you plug away at hearts, declarer will have enough tricks before giving you a seventh trick with your club king). When partner's queen is in spades, there is little hope; declarer will likely put up dummy's king whenever you play your low one (not minding if you have ace–queen; he must guard against the holding you have), and will make his contract with any rational play thereafter.

Clubs offer a better chance. Assuming partner has a second heart, you can defeat the contract any time he has the queen or clubs: shift to the king of clubs. Declarer cannot win lest you later get to partner with the club queen for a heart lead through. When declarer lets you hold the club king, you revert to hearts; now you get your seven tricks before declarer gets his. This shift risks overtricks, but it is the best chance to defeat the contract. There is a fair probability that partner has the club queen, so the risk is worthwhile.

Results

If you bid two hearts, minus 50. Otherwise, if you shifted to the club king, plus 50 (100 if you doubled); if not, minus 90 (180 if you doubled).

Board 2

RHO is the dealer
Your side vulnerable

> **DUMMY (LHO)**
> ♠ 7642
> ♡ 52
> ◊ A754
> ♣ 962

YOU
♠ QJ8
♡ 84
◊ Q108
♣ 108543

RHO	YOU	LHO	PARTNER
2♣	Pass	2◊	Pass
2♡	Pass	2NT	Pass
3♣	Pass	3♡	Pass
3♠	Pass	4◊	Pass
6♡	Pass	Pass	Pass

You lead the spade queen. Declarer thinks for several minutes, then the play goes:

> *Spade queen, deuce, five, **ace**.*
> *Club **king**, three, deuce, seven.*
> *Heart **ace**, four, deuce, three.*
> *Heart **king**, eight, five, six.*
> *Heart **queen**, ?*

Plan your defense.

```
                    NORTH
                    ♠ K53
                    ♡ 10963
                    ◊ J9632
                    ♣ 7
      WEST                          EAST
      ♠ 7642                        ♠ A109
      ♡ 52                          ♡ AKQJ7
      ◊ A754                        ◊ K
      ♣ 962                         ♣ AKQJ
                    SOUTH
                    ♠ QJ8
                    ♡ 84
                    ◊ Q108
                    ♣ 108543
```

There are two ways to solve this difficult problem. One way, which we might call the long cut, is to deduce certain general characteristics of declarer's hand from the bidding and early play.

Partner's play to trick one marks declarer with at least two spades. If the five was low, declarer holds the three; if high, declarer holds the nine or ten, otherwise partner could afford a higher spot. Once you decide declarer has a least two spades, therefore at most two diamonds, perhaps a singleton diamond, you will know you can afford to throw a diamond or two. It is essential for you to keep all your clubs (see diagram). After running winners, declarer will have his side down to:

```
      WEST               EAST
      ♠ 7                ♠ 109
      ♡ —                ♡ —
      ◊ A7               ◊ K
      ♣ —                ♣ —
```

Unless you have a club left at this point, there is no defense if declarer reads the position correctly. When someone keeps two diamonds, that someone is down to a singleton spade honor; declarer cashes the king of diamonds, and plays a spade for a stepping–stone. When neither defender keeps two diamonds, dummy's diamonds are good.

The short cut to the winning defense is to ask yourself why declarer played the king of clubs at trick two. The only sensible answer is that he was trying to make it easy for a defender with five clubs to discard one. If declarer had played only trumps, you would have held all your clubs for fear of setting up his fifth card.

Don't feel too bad if you messed up the defense. Declarer's subtle order of cashing his winners deserved to succeed.

Results

If you held all your clubs against the onslaught of all the trumps, a well deserved plus 50; otherwise, minus 980.

Board 3

South dealer
East–West vulnerable

You, South, hold:

♠ 9742   ♡ AQ10   ◇ J52   ♣ 1084

SOUTH	WEST	NORTH	EAST
Pass	1◇	Pass	1♡
Pass	2♡	Pass	4NT
Pass	5♡¹	Pass	6♡
?			

¹ Two aces

Do you or don't you?

```
                    NORTH
                    ♠ QJ103
                    ♡ —
                    ◇ 10863
                    ♣ 97652
    WEST                            EAST
    ♠ K65                           ♠ A8
    ♡ 8643                          ♡ KJ9752
    ◇ AQ94                          ◇ K7
    ♣ A3                            ♣ KQJ
                    SOUTH
                    ♠ 9742
                    ♡ AQ10
                    ◇ J52
                    ♣ 1084
```

We recommend a double.

Most of the time the opposing heart honors will be
split, and you will defeat the contract one trick doubled,
for a small gain. But part of the time both heart honors
will be in front of you; you will defeat the contract two
tricks, a significant gain for the double. This double may
be important if your teammates reach the same contract, or if they manage to stop at five hearts and go
down one. In the latter case, your double turns a team
pickup of 100 (3 imps) into 400 (9 imps), a gain of 6 imps,
worth taking some chances for.

And what are those chances of loss? Slim indeed.
Could both trump honors show up behind you? Not
likely. LHO has already shown up with two aces in his
minimum–range hand; the odds are against his having
been dealt king–jack of hearts as well. Besides, where
does RHO come off bidding Blackwood with one ace and
no trump suit?

Could the double give away the trump position, letting
the slam make when it was going down before? No! They

may redouble and make it once in a blue moon, but they were going to make it undoubled anyway. Declarer's normal play, with king–jack–fourth in dummy opposite five or six small in his hand, is to finesse the jack on the first round.

What about the possibility of a successful switch to six notrump? That could happen. But they haven't made six notrump yet. How likely is it they can bring it off without heart tricks? Near impossible we'd say. And there is the possibility that six notrump doubled will go down more than six hearts doubled.

Results

If you doubled, plus 500; if not, plus 200.

Board 4

West dealer
Both sides vulnerable

As South, you hold:

♠ AQJ107632   ♡ K84   ◇ 9   ♣ K

LHO opens one heart, which is passed round to you.

What call do you make?

A double accomplishes nothing, and may let the opponents back into the auction; you should bid some number of spades. Since only particular minor–suit cards in partner's hand will help you, and he can't know that, how many to bid is guesswork. All numbers from one to four would have supporters; we think three would be a popular choice. One is unappealing to us because it may allow LHO back into the auction in a minor.

However many spades you bid, everyone passes.

DUMMY
♠ 85
♡ 32
◇ Q10732
♣ A764

YOU
♠ AQJ107632
♡ K84
◇ 9
♣ K

LHO leads the diamond king (five from RHO), and shifts to spade four: five, king, ace.

Nine tricks are easy. Plan the play for ten tricks.

NORTH
- ♠ 85
- ♡ 32
- ◇ Q10732
- ♣ A764

WEST
- ♠ 4
- ♡ AQ1097
- ◇ AKJ4
- ♣ QJ5

EAST
- ♠ K9
- ♡ J65
- ◇ 865
- ♣ 109832

SOUTH
- ♠ AQJ107632
- ♡ K84
- ◇ 9
- ♣ K

Since East had the king of spades, he won't have the ace of hearts. One chance for a tenth trick, therefore, is to try to ruff a heart in dummy. That won't be possible if West has the missing trump; assume East has it.

It is essential to stop East from leading that trump. You can lead hearts safely from the South hand once— the king. But the first heart lead must come from dummy. This will prevent East from gaining the lead when he has only one heart that beats the eight (or when he makes a mistake).

So, enter dummy with the ace of clubs, and lead a heart, covering East's card. Later, you lead the highest heart you have left in the South hand, and, if you are lucky, West will have to win the that one also. You will get your heart ruff, to make ten tricks.

However, the best play for ten tricks is simply to run all the trumps, keeping two diamonds and two clubs in dummy. Declarer may have to guess what to do, but will almost always guess right. One possible plan: If West blanks the heart ace, declarer exits with a low heart, pitching dummy's ace of clubs. Otherwise, declarer leads the club king. If West now blanks the heart ace, declarer lets his club king win, then leads a heart, discarding the club ace. If West keeps two hearts and the ace of diamonds for his last three cards, declarer overtakes the club king, to lead a diamond from dummy.

Results

If you planned the squeeze correctly (you would guess right) or if you finessed your eight of hearts, ten tricks (plus 170 or 620); otherwise, nine tricks (plus 140 or minus 100). If you bid 'em up, you have to play 'em up.

Board 5

North dealer
North–South vulnerable

You, South, hold:

♠ J73   ♡ Q8762   ◇ 3   ♣ K865

SOUTH	WEST	NORTH	EAST
—	—	1♠	Double
2♠	Double[1]	Pass	3◇
?			

[1] Responsive

What call do you make?

Even though it is always tempting to continue the fight when you have a singleton in the opponents' suit, there are many indications that pass is best here. Most important, your spades are short; you should seldom reraise with only three trumps, regardless of other features. Furthermore, your trumps are weak, so you might get doubled. On top of that, you have "soft" values in the off–suits, and the opponents are at the three level—all this suggests defense. And on this vulnerability there is no profit, not even a small one, in going down one at three spades.

You pass three diamonds, and so does everyone else.

What is your opening lead?

```
                     NORTH
                     ♠ AK862
                     ♡ 103
                     ◇ Q965
                     ♣ A7
      WEST                           EAST
      ♠ Q1054                        ♠ 9
      ♡ A54                          ♡ KJ9
      ◇ K104                         ◇ AJ872
      ♣ 1093                         ♣ QJ42
                     SOUTH
                     ♠ J73
                     ♡ Q8762
                     ◇ 3
                     ♣ K865
```

On this auction, it is typical for dummy to be balanced, and for declarer to be short in spades. There is no special reason to lead a trump, and every reason to start spades.

If declarer does have a singleton spade, and often even when he doesn't, it will be advantageous, on balance, to lead the jack. Yes, on occasion declarer will have some annoying singleton honor. But far more often his singleton will be below the jack; then, the high lead will often gain and almost never lose.

Results

This is the sort of deal on which there is a big difference between single–dummy and double–dummy (both are interesting). For match purposes if you bid three spades, minus 100. If you defended against three diamonds and led the spade jack, plus 50; but if you led anything else, minus 110.

Board 6

RHO is the dealer
Opponents vulnerable

DUMMY (LHO)
♠ 107
♡ 963
◇ A53
♣ AQ943

YOU
♠ K9864
♡ AJ
◇ QJ1087
♣ 2

RHO	YOU	LHO	PARTNER
1♣	1♠	3♣[1]	Pass
3NT	Pass	Pass	Pass

[1] Limit

You lead the diamond queen (wouldn't you?), to the ace, deuce and six. Next comes the heart three from dummy, deuce, ten, ?

Plan your defense.

NORTH
♠ 532
♡ KQ542
◇ 42
♣ 765

WEST
♠ 107
♡ 963
◇ A53
♣ AQ943

EAST
♠ AQJ
♡ 1087
◇ K96
♣ KJ108

SOUTH
♠ K9864
♡ AJ
◇ QJ1087
♣ 2

Anyone might have let your sneaky RHO slip the slam by on Deal 2. But this time don't let him do it. The clues stand out boldly, and they do not lead to complex secondary squeezes. Why is declarer who obviously has the king of diamonds killing his own entry to dummy, and not attacking clubs? Either clubs are solid, or the king is missing and he is trying to knock out your entry first. But if he is going after your entry, he wouldn't be playing the ten of hearts at trick two. So declarer has seven minor–suit tricks, plus the spade ace for eight. What's happening in hearts? Declarer would never play this way with king–queen–ten. Could he be finessing hearts from, say, king–ten–eight? Unlikely! He can't expect a fast trick, and the defense will get the diamonds going. Besides, he could run clubs and pulverize your hand—he must suspect he can do that, since you bid spades but led diamonds.

After eliminating the impossible, what remains? You see it in the diagram. Declarer's play is not far–fetched at all. He knows that when he attacks spades, for his ninth trick, the defense will be drawn to hearts as the only chance. It was a good shot to put the problem to the defense immediately. Declarer could have been luckier in the lie of the cards—the winning defense would be much harder if South had ace–queen of hearts.

Results

If you won the ace of hearts, and led anything but a spade, plus 100. Otherwise, minus 600.

Board 7

South is the dealer
Both vulnerable

NORTH
♠ AKJ642
♡ —
♢ AKQ9
♣ A75

SOUTH
♠ 753
♡ AK87
♢ 632
♣ 832

SOUTH	WEST	NORTH	EAST
Pass	Pass	2♣	Pass
2♠[1]	Pass	3♠	Pass
4♠	Pass	5♢	Pass
5♠	Pass	6♣	Pass
6♠	Pass	Pass	Pass

[1] One ace and one king

Do you approve of partner's bidding?

If North had a trump–asking–bid available, he should have used it. Assuming no such action was available, North's percentage action was to bid seven, not six. Opposite three little spades, this would depend on a two–two trump break, a 40% chance; but South might have the ten (sometimes allowing the contract to make against a singleton queen) or four small spades.

Even if this does not bring the grand slam up to the required "standard odds," it is a good risk to bid seven when if seven does not make six may not make either. Technically, the key question is whether seven will have a high enough chance compared to the probability of making six.

West leads the ten of spades to dummy's ace and East's queen.

How do you proceed?

What you should not do is play a second trump. There is time for that later if you so choose. Meanwhile, it is safe to test diamonds. If anybody ruffs a high diamond, you're virtually certain to take the rest of the tricks; the defense may ruff prematurely. If diamonds are not three–three, you can rethink the position. When East is short in diamonds you cannot be denied entry to your hand. When West is short in diamonds, and refuses to ruff, you are no worse off than you we before—you can try to split the remaining trumps if you like.

Everyone follows to three high diamonds. Back to the drawing board.

Now that you've thought things over, it's your move.

                        NORTH
                        ♠ AKJ642
                        ♡ —
                        ◊ AKQ9
                        ♣ A75

WEST   EAST
♠ 1098   ♠ Q
♡ Q105   ♡ J96432
◊ J75   ◊ 1084
♣ K1064   ♣ QJ9

                        SOUTH
                        ♠ 753
                        ♡ AK87
                        ◊ 632
                        ♣ 832

It is true that East may have falsecarded from queen–doubleton, say with,

            ♠ Q8   ♡ J96432   ◊ 1084   ♣ Q9.

Then, suppose that you play North's thirteenth diamond, and it holds; now you give up a club, intending to ruff a club in hand. But East has pitched a club also from the hand above, so he scores his eight of spades for the setting trick. And you were cold for seven.

Of course, a second round of trumps before conceding the club would make the slam against the 2–6–3–2 pattern above. But it could lose—see diagram—when East held a singleton trump (and two or three clubs—if East has long clubs with his singleton trump, the slam can always be set), since West plays the third round of trumps when in with the club. After the thirteenth diamond holds, which line, (a) cashing a second trump, or, (b), first giving up a club—is better?

If you try to make this decision on the basis of straight percentages, you will get into a morass: not only whether the singleton or doubleton queen is the more likely, but which trump West would lead from ten–nine, from ten–eight, whether he would lead a trump if his clubs were headed by king–queen, by king–queen–jack. It's a mess.

However, to adopt line (a) is to credit East with a brilliant deceptive move in tempo at trick one. (The table action on the trick of the thirteenth diamond is not as reliable, since some huddling is likely on that trick regardless of the opposing holdings.) Now, it is perfectly true that East has already, in this very match, shown himself to be a master of deceit. But those plays, good as they were, occurred when East was declarer, in control of information and tempo. Dropping the queen of spades from queen–and–one without thought, even though indicated by the bidding, the dummy and the opening lead, is a play orders of magnitude more difficult than those deceptions East has already executed. There are some plays to which you simply must pay off.

If you don't let East get you with the spectacular queen from queen–and–one spade, you will forever be going down to his normal defensive plays from normal holdings, just from fear that he is doing you in. You must lose to the tough plays from special holdings, to protect yourself against the normal holdings. Thus, line (b) here is the "percentage play," and the "percentage philosophy" against players capable of spectacular moves. If they can come up with the big play, lose and enjoy it.

This advice does not in any way conflict with the suggestions for overcoming declarer's deception on Deals Two and Six. If you can determine from logical reasoning what the basis of an opponent's thought–out play must or might be, you may sensibly act accordingly. It is when you must choose between normality and fast brilliancy that you should come down on the side of normality, and not let the opponents win when they have done nothing more than follow suit.

Results

If you restrained yourself from playing a second round of trumps until you had played the second round of clubs, plus 1430; otherwise, minus 100.

Post–Mortem

Board 1

Where you had to find a shift to the king of clubs from,

♠ A4   ♡ AJ7642   ◇ A8   ♣ K65,

to defeat one notrump, your teammates opened with a 16–18 notrump. The player with your cards overcalled two hearts, passed out, and a well guessed opening lead of a diamond, with careful defense thereafter, defeated the contract (it can be made, double–dummy).

North–South minus 50.

Board 2

Where you had a difficult defense to stop a slam making on a stepping–stone, your teammates bid more conservatively:

OPENER	RESPONDER
♠ A109	♠ 7642
♡ AKQJ7	♡ 52
◇ K	◇ A754
♣ AKQJ	♣ 962

OPENER	RESPONDER
2♣	2♡[1]
3♡	3NT
Pass	

[1] 2 controls

A diamond was led, isolating declarer in dummy (Opener).

North–South minus 460.

Board 3

Where you held ace–queen–ten of trumps against six hearts, your teammates bid somewhat more scientifically (though not all that much more):

OPENER	RESPONDER
♠ K65	♠ A8
♡ 8643	♡ KJ9752
◇ AQ94	◇ K7
♣ A3	♣ KQJ

OPENER	RESPONDER
1◇	1♡
2♡	4NT
5♡[1]	Pass

[1] Two key cards; no heart queen.

North–South plus 100.

Do these hands belong in slam?

Yes. The normal play in hearts (low towards responder's hand, intending to cover the ten with the jack) will pick up the suit with one loser any time the queen is onside, and also when singleton ace is onside. This is more than a 60% chance; 50–50 is okay for slam at IMPs.

Board 4

Where you held,

♠ AQJ107632   ♡ K84   ◊ 9   ♣ K,

the player with your cards reopened on heart with three spades, which was passed out.

```
                    NORTH
                    ♠ 85
                    ♡ 32
                    ◊ Q10732
                    ♣ A764
    WEST                            EAST
    ♠ 4                             ♠ K9
    ♡ AQ1097                        ♡ J65
    ◊ AKJ4                          ◊ 865
    ♣ QJ5                           ♣ 109832
                    SOUTH
                    ♠ AQJ107632
                    ♡ K84
                    ◊ 9
                    ♣ K
```

Your Westmate led the king of diamonds, then shifted to a club. Declarer won in hand, and led the king of hearts (to maximize the chance that the first spade lead would come from West). West won, and tried ace of diamonds. Declarer ruffed, led a heart to East's jack, won the trump return with the ace, and ruffed a heart in dummy. North–South plus 140.

Board 5

Here, you had to find the lead of the spade jack from jack–third to beat three diamonds.

NORTH
♠ AK862
♡ 103
◇ Q965
♣ A7

WEST
♠ Q1054
♡ A54
◇ K104
♣ 1093

EAST
♠ 9
♡ KJ9
◇ AJ872
♣ QJ42

SOUTH
♠ J73
♡ Q8762
◇ 3
♣ K865

SOUTH	WEST	NORTH	EAST
—	—	1♠	Double
2♠	2NT	Pass	Pass
Pass			

Declarer (West) won the opening lead with the queen of spades, cashed the king of diamonds, and ran the ten of diamonds. Gasp!

North–South minus 120.

Board 6

Where you faced a deceptive play by declarer, who had a
wide open suit at three notrump, your teammates faced
fiercer competition.

NORTH
♠ 532
♡ KQ542
◇ 42
♣ 765

WEST
♠ 107
♡ 963
◇ A53
♣ AQ943

EAST
♠ AQJ
♡ 1087
◇ K96
♣ KJ108

SOUTH
♠ K9864
♡ AJ
◇ QJ1087
♣ 2

SOUTH	WEST	NORTH	EAST
–	–	–	1♣
1♠	2♣¹	2♠	2NT
3◇	Pass	3♠	Double
Pass	Pass	Pass	

¹ Inverted

The defense could have made things hot for declarer,
but didn't because West made the "safe" lead of a heart.
Declarer won in hand, and led the queen of diamonds to
East's king. East shifted to clubs. Declarer ruffed the
second round, and played another diamond to West's
ace. Then a club ruffed, a heart to dummy, and a spade
towards the king.

East misdefended at this point by rising with the spade ace. (The defense can get another trick with exact play: East must begin by withholding his spade ace, then must exit with specifically a diamond if South ducks.)

North–South minus 100.

Board 7

Where you were struggling to make six spades, they reached seven at the other table.

NORTH
♠ AKJ642
♡ —
◇ AKQ9
♣ A75

WEST
♠ 1098
♡ Q105
◇ J75
♣ K1064

EAST
♠ Q
♡ J96432
◇ 1084
♣ QJ9

SOUTH
♠ 753
♡ AK87
◇ 632
♣ 832

SOUTH	NORTH
Pass	2♣
2◇	2♠
3♠	4◇
4♡	5◇
5♡	7♠
Pass	

Your teammates had been striking at the ball erratically up to this point in the match but here your East delivered a killing blow. A heart sounded safe on the auction, but he led the queen of spades!

North–South minus 200.

□   □   □

This match turned out to be a much greater challenge than you had any right to expect. Were you up to it?

Match Eight

Once a Year Day

THE DISTRICT REGIONAL IS THE BIG EVENT of the year in your area, especially for those who don't go to the Nationals. Loyal supporter of the local bridge activities that you are, you have played every day of the extended weekend. You have had pretty good games, always well above average, some section firsts and seconds, eleventh overall in the Masters Pairs.

The Swiss is your last chance for something big. But your team is not one of your strongest ever. At the other table you have a pair that scores decently in club events, but often gets eaten up by unfamiliar strong players. Your partner is pleasant, but limited in scope—his play is never really terrible, never really good. At least you have confidence in your partnership, since you know from past experience that partner sticks close to Bridge World Standard, and you have discussed many areas not covered by the basic system.

In this eight–round event, there are more than one hundred teams. (A secondary room had to be hired for the side game.) Scoring is by quarter points: one point for winning (zero for losing) a seven–board match by more than 2 imps; three–quarters for winning (one–quarter for losing) by 1 or 2 imps; half a point for an exact tie.

Things start well. You win three rather close matches against ordinary teams, then get clobbered by a good team. 3–1 at the dinner break. After dinner, you get a little lucky. In the fifth match, the only big swing comes on a game you make with a squeeze, a squeeze broken up, fortuitously, by a different opening lead in the other room. In the sixth match, your strong opponents bid a game and a slam depending on finesses; your side doesn't reach them. Both finesses lose, so your team wins easily. It's not beautiful, but it counts. Things are getting interesting After six matches, the team that beat you is 6–0: they have to play a team with 5–3/4. Two other teams have 5–1; you must play one of them now. A few teams have four–and–a–fraction, but you can't worry about them since you are busy working out that it is possible, if everything goes just right, for your team to win the event outright. Pleasant dreams!

Your opponents for the seventh match are three experts, plus a paying client of unknown caliber. The experts aren't international stars, but they're good enough. Their anchor pair is at your table, and you yourself will sit in the same seat as the third expert at the other table. Your partner figures to outplay the sponsor, and you will do the best you can.

Board 1

Partner is the dealer
None vulnerable

PARTNER	RHO	YOU	LHO
Pass	Pass	Pass	1 ◊
2 ♣	Double[1]	Pass	3 ◊
Pass	3 ♠	Pass	3NT
Pass	4 ♣	Pass	5 ◊
Pass·	6 ◊	Pass	Pass
Pass			

[1] Negative

DUMMY (RHO)
♠ 97542
♡ K53
◊ K
♣ A1062

YOU
♠ K10863
♡ A874
◊ J87
♣ 7

Partner leads the queen of spades.

When should you start thinking about the defense? What general problems should you think about?

Start now! It's never too early. On most hands, you get to take your time in a crucial situation without giving anything away. However, on some hands it will be fatal to be caught thinking at the wrong time. It's virtually impossible to tell, at the outset, which hand is which. So, start thinking right away, just in case there is no time later.

On this deal, you should be thinking about (a) Under what conditions will you take your ace of hearts, if given the opportunity? (b) What will you play if and when you do take it?

The play proceeds:

> *Spade queen, deuce, three, **ace**.*
> *Diamond deuce, three, **king**, seven.*
> *Spade four, six, **diamond four**, jack.*

Are you thinking?

> ***Diamond ace**, ten, spade five, eight.*

There are several essentially different holdings declarer can have, where your plays might matter. Do you know what they are?

Declarer leads the diamond queen. Partner is reaching for his discard.

Are you ready? For anything?

NORTH
♠ QJ
♡ J106
♢ 103
♣ QJ9543

WEST
♠ A
♡ Q92
♢ AQ96542
♣ K8

EAST
♠ 97542
♡ K53
♢ K
♣ A1062

SOUTH
♠ K10863
♡ A874
♢ J87
♣ 7

Are you ready for declarer's lead of the heart jack or ten? Good. But not good enough.

Declarer's spade and diamond holdings are known absolutely. He surely has the king or queen of clubs for his three–notrump bid, so partner has at best a disgusting overcall. Partner must have six clubs, then, so declarer's stopper must be the king. If declarer also holds the club queen or jack, and if he needs the trick, he will unblock his clubs and try to enter dummy with the heart king (which will surely look to him like an entry, on the bidding). In that scenario you will capture the king of hearts with the ace (holding up if declarer leads the queen from his hand).

When declarer has king–small of clubs, with 1–3–7–2 pattern, he likely holds the queen of hearts for his bidding. But maybe not. When he has jack–ten–nine, you can't beat him. When he has jack–ten–small, he will soon run the jack or ten. If partner ducks, you must duck also to have any chance of defeating the contract (else partner will be subjected to a heart–club squeeze). If partner covers with the heart queen, it is safe for you to take the ace (it might cost to duck the ace—in the unlikely event that declarer plays you for it).

The final possibility, which will occur on the actual deal, Is that declarer will start hearts by leading small to dummy's king. To give yourself the best chance to beat the contract, you must duck. And smoothly.

Consider the possibilities. Even if declarer lacks the heart queen (unlikely), he still can't take twelve tricks after your duck, without help. When, as expected, declarer does have the heart queen, you can't beat him if he has the jack. However, as a practical matter your duck will beat him any time he doesn't have the jack. When the heart king holds in dummy, the bidding and play will convince declarer that North, the overcaller, has the heart ace. North can be squeezed. Declarer ruffs a spade and runs his trumps, leading to:

WEST	EAST
♠ —	♠ —
♡ Qx	♡ 53
◇ 6	◇ —
♣ K8	♣ A106

The size of the spot cards is irrelevant, assuming declarer knows the count. He leads his last trump. North must keep three clubs, thus only one heart. Now, declarer can continue with a low heart, dropping North's (hypothetical) ace. On the actual lie of the cards, though, this play will fail.

What do you gain by ducking the heart ace? When declarer started with queen–six–two, he was down anyway. (In fact, if partner follows with the heart nine on the lead to dummy, it might be prudent to win the ace and return a low heart.) When declarer's "x" of hearts in the last diagram is the ten, it is not clear what would happen should you take the ace of hearts—declarer can play either opponent for the heart jack. But when declarer's second–highest heart is the nine you must duck to have any chance. Should you take the ace of hearts, there is just no way for a good declarer to go down: partner is certain to be squeezed.

Win or lose the tournament, if you managed to beat this declarer at this contract you can expect to be playing on stronger teams in the future. But if you *didn't* beat it (and let's face it, most people wouldn't), you must make a strong effort not to let that bother you for the rest of the match. When declarer realizes what might have happened (he may have had the delayed–duck squeeze in mind all along), he may choose to say something starting with "You know, if . . ." Ignore him. Concentrate on the rest of the match.

Results

If you were all set to duck a low–heart lead to the king, plus 50. (You kept only one spade in the ending, for verisimilitude, and you overtook partner's winning heart just to make sure he didn't accidentally exit with a club honor, which would have undone all your good work.) Otherwise, minus 920.

Board 2

East dealer
North–South vulnerable

You, South, hold this beauty:

♠ J85   ♡ 10643   ◇ 752   ♣ 543

PARTNER	RHO	YOU	LHO
Pass	2NT[1]	Pass	7NT
Pass	Pass	Pass	

[1] 21-22

What is your opening lead?

NORTH
♠ 976432
♡ 75
◇ Q6
♣ 1096

WEST
♠ AQ
♡ KQJ
◇ KJ943
♣ 872

EAST
♠ K10
♡ A982
◇ A108
♣ AKQJ

SOUTH
♠ J85
♡ 10643
◇ 752
♣ 543

You can safely ignore all cases in which partner has a jack or less. It is very unlikely, when good opponents bid in this particular manner, that he will have a king. For simplicity, assume that partner has one queen, and no other card above a ten.

Any card you lead in any suit might burn partner's queen, but the best lead is the *jack of spades*. Partner's queen might be in spades, and declarer could pick it up. Thus, he would make his contract because of your lead, but this might happen in all *four* suits. In spades, though, there is a little compensation—the possibility that declarer will choose to finesse you for the ten of spades, and so will lose a cold contract. After all, you might lead from jack–ten, mildly dangerous though it is, to avoid a blind lead that might hit partner's queen.

Even assuming the spade jack lead comes out a little behind (which, by the way, we are *not* conceding). It comes out less behind than anything else. And even if declarer, looking at the spade ten, knows what you have done, he will gain little or nothing. This lead would be even more attractive from a holding such as,

♠ J85   ♡ 10643   ◇ Q52   ♣ 543,

since then you run little risk in the spade suit itself.

Results

If you led a diamond, minus 1520. If you led anything else, plus 50.

Why will declarer go down if you happen to lead a club?

He will eventually decide that if you had a blind guess among worthless holdings for your lead, and if you did not hold the queen of diamonds, you might have chosen to lead a diamond. But you would always choose a different suit when holding the queen of diamonds. Therefore, the odds favor your holding it. (This is a form of restricted–choice argument.)

Why will declarer go down if you lead the jack of spades?

After playing off the rounded suits, he will know you started with four hearts and three clubs. He will presume that you had at most a tripleton spade—who would lead the jack of spades from jack–fourth? Thus, you started with more diamonds than partner. He will have every reason to play you for that queen.

Board 3

DUMMY
♠ J842
♡ 32
◇ 954
♣ A962

YOU
♠ A
♡ KJ109875
◇ AQ102
♣ 4

YOU	LHO	PARTNER	RHO
1♡	Pass	1NT	Pass
4♡	Pass	Pass	Pass

West leads the club king.

This is your first and, almost surely, last chance to lead from dummy.

How do you play?

```
                    NORTH
                 ♠ J842
                 ♡ 32
                 ◇ 954
                 ♣ A962
     WEST                        EAST
  ♠ K1053                     ♠ Q976
  ♡ Q6                        ♡ A4
  ◇ J87                       ◇ K63
  ♣ KQJ10                     ♣ 8753
                    SOUTH
                 ♠ A
                 ♡ KJ109875
                 ◇ AQ102
                 ♣ 4
```

Four lines of play require consideration. A: Lead a heart at trick two, intending to play your king. B: Lead a heart intending to play your jack. (If you lose two trumps, on either line, you will start diamonds by cashing the ace and leading the queen: one loser if either opponent has the singleton king, singleton jack, or doubleton jack.) C: At trick two, lead a diamond, intending to play the queen. D: Lead a diamond, intending to play the ten.

Line A, which picks up ace–doubleton of trumps onside, and singleton queen offside, is better than Line B: that picks up queen–doubleton onside, but not singleton ace offside. As to the choice between diamond finesses, Line C picks up East's singleton king or jack, doubleton king or jack, king–third, king with three or four small, and four little cards. Line D picks up the same singletons and doubletons, also four small; jack–third, on which D works, is exactly as likely as C's king–third. The difference is that jack–fourth or jack–fifth does not replace the king–holdings—declarer still loses two tricks after finessing the ten. So, C is preferable.

Choosing between A and C is more difficult. Line A picks up hearts with one loser slightly under one–third of the time. If that doesn't work, there is still about a one–fifth chance in diamonds: Line A wins a trifle under half the time. Line C would clearly be better than that if the opponents never took a ruff. That long list of diamond holdings given before adds up to about 45%, and there is still the chance of a singleton queen of hearts (you will lead the king from hand, of course)—the total is over 50%.

The chance of a ruff is hard to calculate. It can occur only in a few diamond positions, and then only when the defenders have one of a few specific trump holdings. We think Line C will come out better, but we are not going to work it all out, because it wouldn't prove much. There are limits to how detailed a computation one can preform at the table in practical play.

Results

If you took Line A or C, plus 420. If you took Line B or D (or E—none of the above), minus 50.

Board 4

LHO is the dealer
Both vulnerable

DUMMY
♠ 753
♡ 542
♢ 1064
♣ AQ105

YOU
♠ J42
♡ AKJ87
♢ KQJ
♣ K6

YOU	LHO	PARTNER	RHO
—	Pass	Pass	1♠
2♡	Pass	Pass	Pass

West leads the ten of spades:

> Spade **ten**, three, queen, deuce.
> Spade **ace**, four, nine, five.
> Spade **king**, jack, six, seven.
> Diamond **ace**, jack, three, four.
> Diamond deuce, **king**, five, six.
> Heart **ace**, diamond seven (!), deuce, three.

Whoops!

Plan the play.

NORTH
♠ 753
♡ 542
♢ 1064
♣ AQ105

WEST
♠ 1096
♡ —
♢ 98753
♣ J9872

EAST
♠ AKQ8
♡ Q10963
♢ A2
♣ 43

SOUTH
♠ J42
♡ AKJ87
♢ KQJ
♣ K6

If East started with 4–5–3–1, you can't make it, so you must assume he started with 4–5–2–2. How will the play go? You lead a club to dummy, and play a trump: nine, jack. Now, another club to dummy. This is the ending:

NORTH
♠ —
♡ 5
♢ 10
♣ ??

EAST
♠ 8
♡ Q106
♢ —
♣ —

SOUTH
♠ —
♡ K87
♢ Q
♣ —

At this point, it does no good to lead dummy's last trump (which, in effect, promotes East's eight of spades into a trump); and a diamond will be ruffed. So, it must be a club. Does that work? Not if it's a *losing* club—East will pitch his spade, and get two trump tricks. However, the lead of a club winner from dummy means you're in business. If East discards, you do also—no problem. If East ruffs low, you overruff—no problem. If East ruffs high, you *underruff*—East is endplayed into giving you entry for trump finesse or coup; and you take the rest.

What is the best way to turn dummy's third club into a winner? Your first club play will be the king to the ace. Your next club play depends on where you think the club jack lies. This card would have no effect on the bidding, and probably not on the play, so the odds are 5 to 2 that West has it. The correct play, then, is to handle clubs in this eccentric fashion: first you play your king and ace together; then you finesse against the jack!

An alternative is to play king–ace–queen of clubs at once, succeeding against East's 4–5–2–2 regardless of the location of the club jack. However, this forfeits an extra undertrick when East is 4–5–3–1, and turns out to lead to a small net imp loss in the long run compared to the "funny" line. Observe that East may have been overconfident about the result. If he had exited with a club, he might have had a better chance to defeat you.

Results

If you played as recommended, or played three high clubs immediately, plus 110; otherwise, minus 100.

Board 5

Partner is the dealer
Your side vulnerable

DUMMY
♠ QJ10943
♡ Q6
◇ 103
♣ A98

YOU
♠ 862
♡ K872
◇ A96
♣ 1053

YOU	LHO	PARTNER	RHO
—	—	Pass	1NT[1]
Pass	4♡[2]	Pass	4♠
Pass	Pass	Pass	

[1] 16–18
[2] Transfer to spades

You lead the club three: eight, king, seven. Partner returns the club deuce. Declarer thinks for about fifteen seconds, then wins with the club queen. He leads the five of hearts.

Do you play your king? If so, partner plays the heart nine. What now? If not, how do you plan the defense?

To begin you should play the king of hearts. You have to guard against declarer's holding a hand of this type:

♠ AK   ♡ Axxx   ◇ Qxxx   ♣ QJx

Declarer would have little hope of getting anywhere by attacking diamonds–he can't hope to find your partner, who passed originally, with the king of hearts and ace–king of diamonds. It is a decent shot, though, to try a little heart. You may be tempted to play low with the hand you have (were you?). And if you held the diamond king, you might duck, hoping that the partner had the heart ace–in which case it might be necessary to get the first diamond from his side. However, this is the actual deal:

NORTH
♠ 75
♡ A943
◇ J87
♣ K642

WEST
♠ QJ10943
♡ Q6
◇ 103
♣ A98

EAST
♠ AK
♡ J105
◇ KQ542
♣ QJ7

SOUTH
♠ 862
♡ K872
◇ A96
♣ 1053

It might be nice if partner's signal on the trick you won with the king of hearts showed his *attitude* towards that suit. However, most would play (sensibly, in the general case) that this card, if it shows anything special, shows count. So, partner's heart nine probably says that he has even number of hearts, likely four.

What now? You need to find partner with one prime card—spade ace, heart ace, or diamond king—to defeat the contract. It's not the spade ace, since declarer would then have given up a straightforward play for his contract, establishing a diamond winner for a heart pitch, trying instead for an unlikely deceptive play, which needs a favorable lie of the cards even to have a reasonable chance. Good players just don't do that. Scratch that possibility.

But the other two cases are both within reason. We have seen that declarer might well play like this missing the ace–king of *diamonds*. And his play isn't bad with the hand shown in the diagram either. After all, if he attacks diamonds, the play of that suit is sure to give the defense the clue to cash heart tricks.

How can you guard against both possibilities? Shift to a *low diamond*. If partner has the diamond king, he will win it and return a diamond. If declarer has it, he will win the diamond, but the defense will be in no danger of losing its red–suit aces. Note that it is not adequate to shift to the ace of diamonds, expecting to be able to read partner's signal. Yes, this would be an attitude signal, but the spot cards may be ambiguous (see diagram).

Results

If you ducked the heart, or won and continued hearts, plus 50 (and a black mark). If you won the heart and underled the ace of diamonds, plus 50 (with full honor). If you did anything silly, such as heart king then diamond ace (you'd surely continue diamonds, whichever one partner played), minus 420.

Board 6

East dealer
East–West vulnerable

You, South, hold:

    ♠ 73   ♡ A62   ◇ AKQ2   ♣ J1065

East passes, you open one diamond, West passes and partner responds one heart. East now overcalls one spade.

What call do you make?

The opponents are in position to shut you out with spade raises, so you can't afford to pass. Two clubs suggests a minor two–suiter, which you don't have; and you will find it hard to support hearts later if the opponents bid more spades. Two hearts is the obvious move. You have ample support (considering the ruffing value); the bare possibility that partner has a weak four–card suit should not discourage you. He will often be long. If he has only four hearts, they may be good, or at least fair.

You bid two hearts; LHO competes to two spades: pass, pass, back to you.

What call do you make?

```
                    NORTH
                    ♠ K98
                    ♡ J1098
                    ◊ 54
                    ♣ Q743
      WEST                        EAST
      ♠ AJ5                       ♠ Q10642
      ♡ Q43                       ♡ K75
      ◊ 10976                     ◊ J83
      ♣ K82                       ♣ A9
                    SOUTH
                    ♠ 73
                    ♡ A62
                    ◊ AKQ2
                    ♣ J1065
```

No one knows for sure what is right in these situations. Most theoreticians would suggest a pass (balanced hand, defensive strength, no assured eight–card fit). Many practical players would bid (it never seems to work well to let the opponents play two spades, when they have eight or more trumps). So, you pay your money and take your choice. If you bid, the only sensible option is three clubs, giving partner the maximum selection of strains for your three–level contract. He may think you have 1–3–5–4 and may the chose the wrong red suit, but that's part of the price you pay for . . .

We interrupt this match for a commercial message, brought to you by the weak notrump. Readers, this is the type of deal that demonstrates the merit of the weak notrump. When the strength is spread around fairly evenly, one notrump usually becomes the final contract—and it usually makes, even when it is not a good contract, even if your side had a better contract. Sure, some East may bid on a hand such as this and survive. But sometimes East will be punished for his rashness, as when North holds West's hand, with the nines of spades and diamonds switched: a possible minus 1100 on a part–score deal. Even an occasional 800 or 500 will have its effect on an opponent's future balancing. Yes, the notrumper will himself will go for a number, on very rare occasions. At least, though, he won't face extended rebid problems with balanced hands.

Results

This time, when you take your life in your hands and bid a third time with your weak notrump, it all works out. If you bid three clubs, plus 110. If you passed, minus 110. If you doubled (back to your Ivory Tower!), minus 470.

What's that? You think you can beat two spades? Single–dummy? We doubt it. What about double–dummy? That's a more interesting proposition—more about it later.

Board 7

You are the dealer
Both vulnerable

DUMMY
♠ K10
♡ 8765
♢ K1062
♣ 974

YOU
♠ QJ54
♡ A32
♢ Q854
♣ 62

PARTNER	RHO	YOU	LHO
—	—	Pass	3NT[1]
Pass	Pass	Pass	

[1] Solid minor, one side stopper

Partner leads the heart king.

What do you play?

You should play the three, to encourage as best you can. You can't afford to overtake; partner might have king–queen–jack–fourth, or king–queen–ten–fourth, or maybe king–queen–third.

You play the three, and declarer follows with the nine. Partner continues with the heart ten.

What do you play?

Now you have to overtake—partner would have to play higher than that to get you to keep your ace.

You win the heart ace, and declarer plays the spade seven. Happy days are here again! Nonetheless, your problems on this deal have only just begun.

Plan your defense.

NORTH
♠ 8632
♡ KQJ104
◇ A97
♣ 5

WEST
♠ A97
♡ 9
◇ J3
♣ AKQJ1083

EAST
♠ K10
♡ 8765
◇ K1062
♣ 974

SOUTH
♠ QJ54
♡ A32
◇ Q854
♣ 62

It would be silly to play back anything except a heart, but what are you going to discard on partner's last two heart tricks? Your objective should be to prevent partner from underleading an ace where declarer has no guess. You should give an encouraging attitude signal in a pointed suit in which you hold the ace, or where you have the queen without the jack. You must not be wishy–washy. To discard one club and one spade or diamond would be wrong for two reasons: partner might be unable to read it with certainty; and you would not discard that way if you held an ace, yet you want to make your queen look as much like the ace as possible.

All right, then, no wishy–washy signals. Your discards can be: high–low in diamonds; or, high in diamonds, low in spades, or (not at all the same), low in spades, high in diamonds; or, low–high in spades.

Which of these would you choose if you held the *ace* of diamonds? Probably the last, since you might want to keep all your diamonds in case declarer went wrong. Well, if you'd discard that way with the ace, you should also discard that way with the queen. Like a bluff at poker, a deceptive play against a good player will succeed only when you can make it look just like the alternative possibility—and not always even then.

Which of the six possible low—high spade discards should you use? There is a good chance that all will lead to the same result, but we have a slight preference for the spectacular jack—then—queen, which may, ever so slightly, give the impression of lots of diamonds. This might even embolden partner to underlead ace—jack—third successfully!

One more thing. Are you wondering why to bother with all this when only extra undertricks are at stake? A difference of 100 or 200 could be significant. Even if the earlier boards suggest that the match isn't close enough for this small amount to matter, it is your obligation to do your best. You can never predict with assurance the results of the other boards. The hallmark of a serious player is that he puts forth maximum effort regardless of the situation. If it doesn't matter for the match, it should for personal pride.

Results

If you used any discarding strategy other than the four discussed, plus 200: partner cashed out. If you used one of the first three, plus 100: declarer threw spade seven, diamond three, spade nine, club ten from his hand, and the diamond deuce (an interesting play!) from dummy; stiffening his backbone, partner underled his diamond ace; but you didn't fool declarer, and he guessed right. If you pitched low—high in spades, plus 300.

Post–Mortem

Board 1

Where you faced an extraordinarily difficult defensive position against six diamonds, your teammates quite sensibly stopped at game.

NORTH
♠ QJ
♡ J106
◇ 103
♣ QJ9543

WEST
♠ A
♡ Q92
◇ AQ96542
♣ K8

EAST
♠ 97542
♡ K53
◇ K
♣ A1062

SOUTH
♠ K10863
♡ A874
◇ J87
♣ 7

WEST	NORTH	EAST	SOUTH
—	Pass	Pass	Pass
1◇	3♣	3NT	Pass
Pass	Pass		

South led the seven of clubs.

How should declarer (East) have played?

There is no problem if diamonds are 3–2, but what if they are 4–1? Then, declarer will have to unblock the king of diamonds, get to dummy with ENTRY 1, establish diamonds, and later return to dummy with ENTRY 2 to run the rest of the suit. It is too dangerous to try to use the heart queen as ENTRY 1. Either opponent might win with the ace and establish the setting tricks in spades or hearts. Similarly, using the spade ace as ENTRY 1 is foolhardy—the defense might get three spades, one heart, one diamond. So, the club king should be ENTRY 1. That's safe. The play should go: club seven–eight–jack –ace; diamond king; club king; diamonds.

In practice, declarer, your teammate, led a heart at trick three, losing nothing on the lie of the cards.

North–South minus 460.

Board 2

Where seven notrump depended on locating the queen of diamonds, the bidding in the other room also went two notrump–seven notrump (we think West should, instead, produce a sequence that allows him to check for the diamond queen).

NORTH
♠ 976432
♡ 75
◇ Q6
♣ 1096

WEST
♠ AQ
♡ KQJ
◇ KJ943
♣ 872

EAST
♠ K10
♡ A982
◇ A108
♣ AKQJ

SOUTH
♠ J85
♡ 10643
◇ 752
♣ 543

Here, South led the six of hearts. Your teammate, East, played off all his heart, club and spade winners, reducing everyone to three cards. He then misguessed diamonds, finessing through South, losing the last two tricks.

North–South plus 100.

Did this declarer do anything wrong?

His unhappy misguess in diamonds was not clearly wrong, although North's heart shortness might have steered declarer right, but for the wrong reason. However, it was an error for him to cash the second round of spades. Nothing was going to happen on that trick to change his mind about diamonds, so the only effect was to risk a second undertrick.

Board 3

Where you had to decide how to make best use of your only dummy entry at four hearts, the bidding in the other room went one heart, all pass. Declarer won the opening club lead in dummy, and led a trump to his jack, eventually making nine tricks. That result surprises you slightly, though you can't think why . . .

North–South plus 140.

Board 4

Where you struggled in two hearts against a 5–0 trump break, your teammates made the running at the other table.

NORTH
♠ 753
♡ 542
◇ 1064
♣ AQ105

WEST
♠ 1096
♡ —
◇ 98753
♣ J9872

EAST
♠ AKQ8
♡ Q10963
◇ A2
♣ 43

SOUTH
♠ J42
♡ AKJ87
◇ KQJ
♣ K6

East opened a Flannery two diamonds in third position (four spades, five hearts, a minimum–range opening). West converted to two spades. North defended effectively. He started well by leading a trump. Declarer (West) won in dummy, ruffed a heart, played a diamond to the ace, ruffed another heart, and exited with a diamond to South's queen. South took the club king, led a club to partner. North shifted to hearts: South cashed three heart winners. However, North *ruffed* the fifth round of hearts, to play another club, promoting South's spade jack.

North–South plus 200.

Board 5

Your teammates nearly produced a big result.

NORTH
♠ 75
♡ A943
◇ J87
♣ K642

WEST
♠ QJ10943
♡ Q6
◇ 103
♣ A98

EAST
♠ AK
♡ J105
◇ KQ542
♣ QJ7

SOUTH
♠ 862
♡ K872
◇ A96
♣ 1053

SOUTH	WEST	NORTH	EAST
—	—	Pass	1NT
Pass	3♠	Pass	3NT
Pass	Pass	Pass	

South lead the deuce of hearts, "Journalist," the lowest card against a notrump contract to suggest continuing the suit, without giving count. Declarer (East) played the six from dummy, and captured North's nine with the jack.

Was North's play of the nine brilliance, blunder or between?

Brilliance! North recognized the advantage of concealing the heart count from declarer. One possible approach was for him to win the heart ace and return the "wrong" spot card, but this might confuse partner. Alternatively, North could play back the "right" card (the three), and hope that declarer plays him to be trickily returning the wrong spot—but declarer would scarcely believe that North would risk confusing South.

By playing his nine, North avoided these complexities. This eliminated the necessity of returning anything; it concealed the exact count, and made declarer think that the lead was away from the ace–king (which also suggested a long suit). Was there any risk? Not really. Declarer was marked with at least three hearts on the bidding; without the jack, he would presumably have put up dummy's queen at trick one.

Declarer unblocked his spade honors, learning little. Then, he had to take a view about the hearts. If hearts were 5–3, the club finesse was the only real hope; if hearts were 4–4, declarer could afford to knock out the ace of diamonds. After thinking about the suit for a while, even doing some actual counting, declarer took the club finesse. North–South plus 50.

Should declarer have played differently?

Yes! His wrong view was unlucky, but he could have prevented North from posing such a difficult problem; declarer should have put up dummy's queen of hearts. Now North would simply have to play an honor, if he had one, from most holdings. His heart return, even though possibly deceptive, would give declarer more to go on than in the actual case. More important, South would have to play some cards, and might err. At the least, the inexperienced half of the partnership, perhaps unaware of the subtleties of the situation, might provide some dependable intelligence. Declarer would have an unwitting spy in the enemy camp, as it were.

Having determined this, and remembering Board 3, something occurs to you.

"Wasn't the good player sitting in my seat?" you ask.

"They switched after you left," says your East. "Something about the light."

"Next board," says your partner.

Board 6

NORTH
♠ K98
♡ J1098
◇ 54
♣ Q743

WEST
♠ AJ5
♡ Q43
◇ 10976
♣ K82

EAST
♠ Q10642
♡ K75
◇ J83
♣ A9

SOUTH
♠ 73
♡ A62
◇ AKQ2
♣ J1065

The bidding was the same as at your table; two spades was passed around to your hand. Your counterpart passed, so two spades became the final contract.

South led king, queen, ace of diamonds, then a fourth diamond to kill dummy's winner, North ruffed. Declarer, East, overruffed; he lost a spade finesse, let the jack–of–hearts return run around to dummy's queen, and drew trumps with a second round. Declarer knew that South had three hearts, from the bidding; there was no chance to drop the ace doubleton. So, he hoped South had ace–king–queen of diamonds and queen–jack of clubs for his opening bid, giving North the heart ace. Declarer crossed to dummy's club king, and led towards the king of hearts, as his only chance.

North–South plus 50.

Could East have done any better?

East was in there thinking, but not deeply. Aside from the improbability of the holding he was playing for, why would North, with a safe spade exit among others, have switched to hearts? Of course, if there is no other chance . . .

But there is. South is marked with ace–third of hearts. If his low cards are precisely six–deuce, quite a substantial possibility since North should have at least jack–ten–nine to make his heart shift safe, the squeeze is on. Not a routine squeeze, we admit, but East is in effect playing double–dummy. After the fourth round of trumps, this is the position:

NORTH
♠ —
♡ 109
♢ —
♣ Q74

WEST
♠ —
♡ 43
♢ —
♣ K82

EAST
♠ 4
♡ K7
♢ —
♣ A9

SOUTH
♠ —
♡ A6
♢ —
♣ J106

East, who needs four of the last five tricks, leads his last trump; and each opponent is squeezed in turn. South cannot afford to bare his ace of hearts, so he must throw a club. Dummy throws a heart, and North has to keep all his clubs—he must throw a heart. East can now lead the king of hearts (or play a heart after two round of clubs), to make his lucky seven of hearts the contract–going trick. There was nothing to lose by trying for this.

The defense cannot prevail after starting with four rounds of diamonds, even if North then shifts to a club—declarer can win the ace, and reach an equivalent ending. But South can give North his ruff on the *third* diamond; now North can lead low clubs twice—here, and again when on lead with the spade king—to break up the squeeze (the secondary queen–of–hearts entry is not strong enough in the complex position required). Alternatively, South can switch to a club honor after the first diamond. When North wins his trump king, he gets a diamond ruff on the third round, then plays another club (keeping his queen).

Board 7

Where you had a tricky discarding problem against a three–notrump contract already on the way down, the action was as conservative at the other table as it was bold at yours.

SOUTH	WEST	NORTH	EAST
Pass	1♣	Double	Pass
1♠	2♣	Pass	Pass
2♦	3♣	Pass	Pass
Pass			

Declarer guessed right in diamonds, making 11 tricks. North–South minus 150.

□   □   □

The results of other matches in this round went nicely for you. Is your team still in contention?